On the Edge of Your Seat

Chairs for the 21st Century

On the Edge of Your Seat

Chairs for the 21st Century

THE CENTER FOR ART IN WOOD®

4880 Lower Valley Road • Atglen, PA 19310

Contents

Prologue

n an effort to understand more about the history of our field—CRAFTS, and to discover just how far back it really goes, I consulted the Ultimate Authority—the Venus of Willendorf, the magnificent Ghost of Crafts Past. She took me on a tour that began in a cave, circa 2001 B.C. (Before Craft). I took notes of what transpired, and wrote the following play, which reiterates the conversation verbatim and exactly as it took place. I shall narrate and play all the roles myself.

THE CLAN OF
THE CAVE CRAFTS

OR

A TWO-MINUTE HISTORY
OF CRAFT AS WE KNOW IT

Being a Melodrama in two short acts,
and an Extremely Abbreviated History of Craft
that cuts directly to the Good Parts, but in its Brevity,
Spares No Detail.

ACT ONE

SCENE I: A CAVE:

Present are **OG**, *the Hunter-Gatherer,* **OGGA**, *his Significant Other, and* **OGGLY**,
   their Child.

OGGA: "Me tired of sitting on rock. Rock hard."

OG: "Me fix." He exits the cave.

OGGLY: "Me go with." He follows Og out of the cave.

SCENE II: TWO HOURS LATER:

*Og returns carrying a log with little Oggly dangling from one end. Og proudly drops
   the log on the floor of the cave.*

OG: "Sit."

Thus is born the first Craftsman and the first Functional Object.

SCENE II: THE NEXT DAY:

OGGA, *sitting on her log:* "Still too hard."

OGGLY: "Too hard, Poppa!"

Og emits an expletive grunt and exits the cave.

SCENE III: THREE HOURS LATER:

*OG returns bloody and scarred, but with a fresh bear skin, which he throws over
   the log.*

OG: "Sit now."

Thus is born the first Upholstered Functional Object.

SCENE IV: THREE DAYS LATER:

OGGA, *sitting on her newly upholstered log:* "Now everybody in clan want furry
   log like mine."

OG: "Me make."

OGGLY: "Me help."

OGGA: "Me sell. Me collect clams."

*Thus is born the first Entrepreneur, the first Apprentice and the first
   Business Manager.*

ACT TWO

ONE MOON LATER

The rest of the clan is lined up outside of the cave, waiting for their upholstered logs.
    Og, now a huge success, is busily putting pelts on logs and is wearing a pair
    of Italian handmade sandals. Ogga is sitting on her log, counting huge pile
    of clams.

OGGA: "Now everyone will have bear-chair just like mine. Want more special."

OG, *his eyeballs rolled upwards*: "Me fix."

He reaches into his three-piece loincloth and takes out a sharpened stone, with
    which he proceeds to carve an image of a woolly mammoth on Ogga's log:

OG: "Now—special."

OGGA, dreamily: "Ohhh—Og!"

The lights fade, the curtain falls. As a result of Ogga's gratitude, the size of Og's family was doubled. Thus began the History of the Decorative Arts. Oggly and his new sibling More Oggly eventually took over the family craft business. Several moons later, they had a disagreement concerning the division of labor and chores. Oggly moved out of the cave and started selling his upholstered logs in a tent. Thus was born the first Craft Fair. Meanwhile, More Oggly continued to take orders from inside the cave and paid only half to Oggly who was getting tired of camping out. Thus began the first Craft Gallery. Eventually they were reunited, called their business OGGLYWARE, and added more caves. The business was handed down from generation to generation to generation to generation to generation, etc., etc., etc., etc., etc., thus creating the first Crafts Dynasty.

Even though OGGLYWARE is now made in China, the handmade one-of-a-kind studio furniture created by their descendants may still be seen in every major archeology museum throughout the world.

THE END

Roy Superior (1934–2013)

Professor of Art/Wood
Who performed this sketch for his students at University of the Arts, Philadelphia

On the Edge of Your Seat

Chairs for the 21st Century

C hairs are a daily experience for all of us, and most of us treasure our favorite one for its comfort and the sense of well-being it provides. Over the course of American furniture making, the chair has been at the center of furniture arts. The Center for Art in Wood, in conjunction with The Furniture Society, decided to send out a call to artists to design and create chairs to bring us into the twenty-first century.

Responding were 147 artists proposing 251 entries. The jury selected forty-five chairs designed by thirty-nine artists (including six students) for display at the center in an exhibition to be held at the same time as the society's 2016 conference, from June 23 to 25 at the University of the Arts (UArts), cosponsored by UArts and the center. Some chosen works are more conventional than others, but each is an extrapolation that builds on the years of classic chair design with a new twist to assure their contemporary nature. This publication catalogues and explains the work.

The center acknowledges The Furniture Society for its assistance in producing the exhibit as well as for its important work over the years in saluting and developing furniture of all kinds. We thank Steffanie Dotson, its president, for her work and guidance.

We particularly acknowledge the tireless work of the jurors who culled through the presentations to select the work in the show. Each of the jurors has also written an essay to be found in this volume. We thank Nora Atkinson, Lloyd Herman Curator of Craft at the Smithsonian American Art Museum's

Renwick Gallery; Jasper Brinton of Brinton Design in Phoenixville, Pennsylvania; Benjamin Colman, Associate Curator of American Art at the Detroit Institute of Arts; and Susie Silbert of New York, an independent curator, historian, and prolific writer on the arts scene.

We thank Joshua Lane, the Lois F. and Henry S. McNeil Curator of Furniture, Winterthur Museum, Garden & Library, for his illustrated essay on Philadelphia chairs from 1620 through the twentieth century. We thank the artists for their work and the artist statements each prepared. We are grateful to the applicants whose work was not selected but that was nevertheless of high quality.

This book would not be possible without the funding provided by the Fleur Bresler Publication Fund at The Center for Art in Wood. Many thanks to our designer, Dan Saal; our editor, Judson Randall; and Center registrar Karen Schoenewaldt who, with the help of administrative assistant Katie Sorenson, organized all of the entries, which greatly enabled the work of the jury. Thanks to the center's exhibition committee and publication committee for their work on the project.

Of course, the idea for this exhibition was developed by Albert LeCoff, cofounder and executive director of the center. Albert has been and remains the creative genius behind much of what has developed in the field of contemporary wood art. He motivates artists and promotes their art to the highest level.

The board and staff of the center hope that all who see the exhibition or read this publication will understand the inspiration that can motivate the artist to think in new directions and create beautiful and imaginative work using an everyday object such as the chair. These chairs bring the art to a new level.

Richard R. Goldberg
President, The Center for Art in Wood

From The Furniture Society

O n the Edge of Your Seat: Chairs for the 21st Century continues an ongoing partnership between The Center for Art in Wood and The Furniture Society that dates to 2003. In that year, these two organizations—united in passion and complementary in mission—embarked on a collaborative exhibition titled *Cabinets of Curiosities*. At the time, The Center for Art in Wood was operating under its old name, the Wood Turning Center, and its focus was primarily on the tool of the lathe and the concentricity (or studied asymmetry) that it can create. Historically linked, turning and furniture making had drifted apart; *Cabinets of Curiosities*, initiated by the center's Albert LeCoff, created a bridge uniting these disparate disciplines for a contemporary era.

Today, under the organization's new auspices, *On the Edge of Your Seat: Chairs for the 21st Century* highlights a relationship of a different kind: the long-standing and still generative connection between the material of wood and the field of furniture. The forty-plus pieces included in these pages and the exhibition they accompany encompass a breadth of approaches to material, to seating, and to object-making. Set against the backdrop of a contemporary world increasingly invested in mass production and still dependent even in the newest technologies on petroleum-based materials, a world of lowered standards and an elevation of style over substance, these works stand as a beacon to the vitality and critical importance of independent artisans and designers in raising the bar of excellence in the built world.

In its rigorous appraisal of twenty-first-century seating, *On the Edge of Your Seat* does much to further the mission of The Furniture Society. Founded twenty years ago to advance studio furniture making by inspiring creativity, promoting excellence, and fostering understanding of this art and its place in society, we are the preeminent organization advocating on behalf of furniture makers and designers. By sponsoring a variety of programs that contribute to the education and enrichment of members and the public, The Furniture Society champions excellence, refinement, responsibility, and craftsmanship in furniture. In bringing high-quality work to a wide audience across the country, *On the Edge of Your Seat* actively aligns with our mandate to raise the visibility of contemporary furniture, its makers, ideas, and traditions.

This exhibition could not have happened without the tireless efforts of a number of people. Thanks go first and foremost to Albert LeCoff, cofounder and executive director of The Center for Art in Wood, for planting the seeds of this project and diligently nurturing them to fruition. The jurors, Nora Atkinson, Jasper Brinton, Benjamin Colman, and Susie Silbert, have brought a high level of expertise to their selections and to their writings; the show is better for their insightful contributions. A debt of gratitude is also due to the staff of The Center for Art in Wood, in particular Karen Schoenewaldt and Katie Sorenson, who herded jurors and artists alike through the process. And of course, sincere thanks go out to all the makers—both those included in these pages and those who are not: you are the reason for all of this.

Steffanie Dotson
Furniture Society Board President

Introduction

For years, I've fantasized about re-creating the arch of chairs captured in a vintage black-and-white photograph taken in High Wycombe, England. The arch combined many Windsor chairs by local makers in a celebration of a visit by the Prince of Wales in 1884. Philadelphia, where I grew up, is a city of furniture history. Since the 1700s, cabinets and chairs of all types have been designed and made here. The "Rising Sun" chair, made by John Folwell in 1779, was used by George Washington for nearly three months during the Federal Convention's continuous sessions in Philadelphia[1] and is a perfect example of this legacy.

When The Center for Art in Wood moved to Old City, Philadelphia, in 2011, I began to see places to re-create the arch of chairs. Old City has a long history as an industrial neighborhood, and Elfreth's Alley, the oldest continuously inhabited residential block in the United States, housed several Windsor chair makers in the 1700s and 1800s. That narrow alley would be the perfect place for an arch of chairs. Nearby Quarry Street, an alley of Belgian blocks, holds similar potential. At the west end of Quarry Street, The Center for Art in Wood could provide the perfect terminus with a chair exhibition to draw people inside.

One of the most ambiguous furniture forms, chairs lend themselves to many interpretations—symbol, function, sculpture. With the chair arch—and chairs themselves—never far from my mind's eye, the perfect moment to explore chairs on the ground arose. The Furniture Society will hold its annual symposium in Philadelphia in 2016.

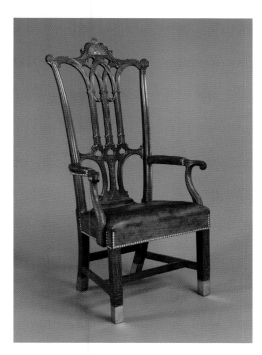

Arch of chairs, built to celebrate the visit of the Prince of Wales to Hughenden, adjacent to the Guildhall, High Sreet, High Wycombe, c. 1880 | Sharing Wycombe's Old Photographs, Bucks Free Press, www.swop.org.uk

John Folwell | *"Rising Sun" Chair,* 1779 | Mahogany | 60½ x 30½ x 22⅞ in. |
Independence National Historic Park | Joseph Elliott

In early 2015, The Center for Art in Wood and The Furniture Society launched a call for chairs on our websites and others, the Internet being the broadest way to reach today's artists. In July 2015, professional jurors enthusiastically reviewed 251 entries from 147 artists and entertained a rigorous discussion to select the field. Viewpoints ranged from curators to makers. At the table with me were Nora Atkinson, Lloyd Herman Curator of Craft at the Smithsonian American Art Museum's Renwick Gallery, Washington, DC; Jasper Brinton, designer and woodworker and principal at Brinton Design, Phoenixville, Pennsylvania; Benjamin Colman, associate curator of American Art at the Detroit Institute of Arts; and Susie Silbert, New York–based curator, writer, and historian.

Chair makers and designers submitted stunning professional photographs, some of the best I've witnessed in forty years of reviewing work. Photographs captured the concepts and beauty that some of the artists created, but the jurors also fielded drawings, paintings, and videos as modern tools of presentation.

From August until November 2015, the artists made, finalized, and submitted their finished works to the center.

With this book and installation, artists present their visions of chairs for the twenty-first century. Thirty-nine artists delight and amuse us with forty-five symbols and sculptures, while historical context informs and increases our appreciation of the contemporary chairs. Thanks to recommendations from furniture aficionado Edward "Ned" Cooke of Yale University, the perfect overview and salute to Philadelphia's iconic chairs is provided by Joshua Lane, the Lois F. and Henry S. McNeil Curator of Furniture, Winterthur Museum, Garden & Library.

The innovative responses to the call for chairs reflect and document our world in the first quarter of the twenty-first century. Responses to the call included drawings, paintings, ink-jet prints, videos, and a chair installation incorporating sound and projected images. Christy Oates's YouTube video is a first; it captures her inspiration and exacting computer-assisted design and execution. Similarly, Amy Forsyth's colorful, detailed proposal was so vibrant that the jurors were ready to accept it with no need for Forsyth to make the real thing. Needless to say, it is part of the installation.

On the Edge of Your Seat: Chairs for the 21st Century offers a range of delights—something for everyone.

The artists' fantasies, methods, and skills vary from traditional hand-carving to lamination to computer-aided design and execution. The chairs include precious one-of-a-kind specimens, multiples such as those by Takahiro Yoshino, and mass-produced beauties by Po Shun Leong. And happily, the student work stands shoulder to shoulder with the professionals. What a tribute to their university programs and to their promising potentials! I wish for each artist continued inspiration, tools, materials, and the places and sales that will help them to continue their work. This exhibition will be a success if all viewers appreciate the skills, toil, and results they witness, and become advocates of contemporary artwork.

I am personally grateful to each partner and funder for lending their special talents to the realization of this project. Maggie Sasso of The Furniture Society was a helpful contact. Judson Randall once again collegially edited this publication from a worn office chair, working to include the essays, the captions, and the continuity for which he stands. Dan Saal of StudioSaal Corporation, in the pilot's seat, steered the design of the book and of the *On the Edge of Your Seat: Chairs for the 21st Century* installation. For over a year, backstage logistics and organization were superbly executed by the center's registrar, Karen Schoenewaldt, from her upholstered office chair. She, along with administrative associate Katie Sorenson, worked side by side with me to facilitate the call, the jurying, the submissions, the database, the installation, and this publication. Thanks to each of you and to all the staff at the center who provide invaluable support for everything we accomplish.

Now, I invite you to please take a seat and enjoy this book.

Albert LeCoff
with Tina C. LeCoff

NOTE

1.   INDE Collections, "The 'Rising Sun' Chair," accessed December 8, 2015. https://indecollections.wordpress.com/2012/09/18/the-rising-sun-chair/.

Chairs and Chairmaking in Philadelphia

A Selective Pictorial History

As attested by the contemporary seating furniture in this book, present-day studio furniture makers are carrying forward a tradition of design excellence and innovation extending back to the seventeenth century. Reflecting its population of ethnically diverse Europeans, comprising English, Irish, Dutch, Swedish, French, and German immigrants, Philadelphia's earliest cabinetmakers and chair makers selectively adapted stylistic elements outside their own received traditions to create distinctive hybrid designs. In the eighteenth century, many drew inspiration from English design books and studied imported furniture to develop designs conceived in the English taste but that also reflected local preferences. By 1772, they had codified various decorative options in a published price guide, updated and reissued on a semiannual basis through the early nineteenth century. Working within the constraints of their clients' desires and the range of style options described in these price books, many craftsmen expressed not only consummate mastery of technique but also a high degree of personal creativity in their best work. The quality and richness of their products impressed leaders from other colonies who convened in Philadelphia to chart the course of the Revolution and shape a new government, and it attracted cabinetmakers and chair makers from the mid-Atlantic, New York City, and as far away as the Connecticut River Valley, seeking to learn the "Philadelphia style" and to replicate it back home. In the nineteenth century, masters of Philadelphia's best furniture shops designed and produced furniture rivaling that of New York's celebrated cabinetmakers. Inspired by the arts and crafts movement in England, a new generation of craftsmen in the early twentieth century returned to limited-production work, pioneering the studio movement. As a prelude to appreciating contemporary seating furniture crafted in Philadelphia, the following selection of chairs features objects that were new and exciting when they were made—some were conceived at the cutting edge of international design trends, others brought familiar design elements together in unique ways. These chairs, and those of Philadelphia craftsmen and furniture firms not represented in this survey, manifest excellence and innovation from earlier times, charting the rich historical context for more deeply appreciating the works of today.

COLONIAL PHILADELPHIA

In the 1620s, the Dutch claimed homelands of the Lenape, Susquehannock, and other Native American communities along the Delaware River as part of New Netherland and established several enclaves of Dutch and Swedish settlers. By 1671, the English had assumed control of New Netherland, and, in 1681, English Quaker William Penn obtained a royal charter from King Charles II granting him a vast tract that he named Pennsylvania. To encourage settlement, Penn enacted a policy of religious freedom, attracting English and Welsh Quakers and Baptists; German Lutherans, Mennonites, and Moravians; Scots-Irish Presbyterians; French Huguenots; and Jews. He planned the market town of Philadelphia as "a Greene Country Towne, wch will never be burnt, and allways be wholsome," patterned in a grid between the Schuylkill and Delaware Rivers. With the development of a deep-water port on the Delaware River, Philadelphia quickly grew into an important shipping hub. By 1750, the city had surpassed Boston to become the largest port in North America and was

The quality and richness of their products impressed leaders from other colonies who convened in Philadelphia to chart the course of Revolution and shape a new government.

second only to London as the biggest city in the British Empire. Penn recruited craftsmen to the city, attracting more than 120 artisans of many ethnicities by 1690. In the structures they built, furniture and other household goods that they made, these craftsmen continually confronted the questions: What identity should they reflect in their designs? What was considered fashionable? Appropriate and true to oneself, one's clients, and the larger community?

Furniture historian Benno Forman identified this low-back side chair (fig. 1), with its walnut twist-turned frame and white oak board seat, as "one of rarest survivals of the framed chair maker's art" from early America. Nearly all of its frame elements are carved with double-twists entirely worked by hand with files and rasps, as evidenced by filemarks in the concavity of each helix. The laborious and time-consuming process of carving the twists added greatly to the expense of this design, and consequently, not many were made. The seat consists of two boards fitted together with a tongue-and-groove joint and slotted into grooves plowed in the sides of the seat rails a half inch below the upper edge. This recessed seat, common in Pennsylvania walnut wainscot chairs modeled after those of northern England, created a shallow well to hold a plump seat cushion. Earlier furniture historians attribute the twist-turn design to chair makers working in the Netherlands or elsewhere in continental Europe. Citing a 1672 bill in the British royal household accounts from London joiner Richard Price for "back Chair frames turned all over wth the twisted turne," Forman noted, however, that spiral-turned seating furniture was fashionable in England. English yeoman Robert Pearson of Crosswicks Creek, New Jersey (absorbed into Hamilton Township and Trenton in the mid-nineteenth century), is thought to have first owned this example, a hybrid of English and Swedish design. In 1925, a closely related example (now at the Philadelphia Museum of Art) was acquired in Hamilton Township. Although it is possible that a rural New Jersey chair maker made these expensive and stylistically sophisticated chairs as part of a larger set, it is likely that they were made in Philadelphia and shipped to their owners via a short boat trip up the Delaware River.

FIG. 1 *Side chair,* 1683–1705 | Black walnut, white oak | 39¼ x 19 x 19¼ in. | Philadelphia, Pennsylvania | Winterthur Museum, gift of Henry Francis du Pont, 1957.1389

Furniture scholar Allan Miller has noted that early Philadelphia turners excelled at their craft, producing robust and inventive designs that raised their work above that of turners elsewhere in the colonies. Of this chair (fig. 2) Benno Forman noted: "The extraordinary balusters on the legs and arm supports ... [place this example] in the exclusive group of furniture masterpieces made in America during its first century of northern European colonization." The carved, molded crest, corresponding lower back rail, and molded stiles form a tall, wide frame for the caned back—caning being a lightweight, luxury imported material available only to the very wealthy. In addition to the use of cane, the large bulbous elements of the arm supports, repeated in the front legs and front stretcher, and the scrolled feet elevated this chair as a fashion-bearing status symbol. In an unusual design innovation, the oversize front leg turnings serve in place of blocks to anchor the front stretcher. Representing the handiwork not only of a turner but also a caner who wove the back and seat and a carver who executed the scroll feet and volute handgrips, this chair exhibits workmanship unique to Philadelphia. The multi-reeded scrolled feet, similar to those on Philadelphia and Germantown case furniture, extend below square blocks cut without rounded shoulders, and the oversize turnings are cut from blocks built out with four glued cheeks. This method enabled the turner to use narrow stock for the workpiece, saving time and materials.

The extraordinary balusters on the legs and arm supports ... [place this example] in the exclusive group of furniture masterpieces made in America during its first century of northern European colonization.

Little evidence has come to light documenting cane chair makers in Philadelphia. Forman noted in the account book of merchant John Reynell a 1721 entry noting Thomas Stapleford's purchase of "Merch[andise] from Britain: for 3 Doz Cane for Chairs." In his will, proved 1739, Stapleford conveyed

FIG. 2 *Armchair* | 1690–1720 | Black walnut, walnut, cane | 43⅞ x 25⅜ x 22⅞ | Winterthur Museum, gift of David H. Stockwell; 1955.130

to his "daughter Elizabeth ... half a dozen Cane Chairs to be finished at the Charge of my Estate by my Executors." It is not clear whether Stapleford worked as a chair maker or caner; in either case, it is unlikely that he made this chair. As a recent arrival from Boston, he would have been familiar with Boston-style cane chairs that differ substantially from this example. Although a brass plate attached to the rear of the crest is inscribed "Chair of Thomas Lloyd, Governor of Pennsylvania 1684–1693," it is likely that one of Lloyd's sons, either Mordecai or Thomas, first owned the chair. Lloyd served as lieutenant governor from 1690 to 1693, before his death in 1694.

This joined armchair (fig. 3) combines a shaped crest drilled with two holes and incised with opposing diagonal lines to define a central floral motif, molded vertical bannisters, and turnings for its visual appeal. Originally, a board seat set into grooves in the seat rails would have been furnished with a cushion. The design for the turning of the front stretcher and arms derives from English practice; the vase-shaped arm support elements scribed at their waists are characteristic of Philadelphia work. The crest and raked-back rear stiles, turned above the seat, feature columnar passages above vase elements that relate to those on a pair of turned side chairs possibly made in Philadelphia (fig. 4). These side chairs also feature two front stretchers turned following a design "first used in French seating during the reign of Louis XIII and that persisted two centuries in areas of French cultural influence, such as Quebec," according to Allan Miller. Based on this stylistic link to traditional French turned seating furniture, Miller raises the possibility that an immigrant Huguenot craftsman such as Solomon Cresson produced these chairs, and, by association, the armchair.

The arc of Solomon Cresson's life exemplifies the movement of craftsmen and intermixing of design ideas that contributed to "creolized" furniture

It is not clear whether Stapleford worked as a chair maker or caner;

in either case, it is unlikely that he made this chair.

FIG. 4 *Pair of side chairs*, 1715–1730 | Maple, ash | Philadelphia, Pennsylvania | Private collection, Pook & Pook | Pook & Pook

FIG. 5 *Armchair*, 1725–1745 | Black walnut, leather | 49⅞ x 24⅞ x 24 in. | Philadelphia, Pennsylvania |
Winterthur Museum, Bequest of Henry Francis du Pont, 1954.518

characteristic of early Philadelphia. Cresson's grandfather, Pierre Cresson, moved from France to Holland, then, with his father, Jacques Cresson, to Harlem, New York, where both were members of the Dutch Reformed church. After Jacques died in 1684, Solomon's mother, Maria Reynard Cresson, moved to Curacao, possibly leaving behind Solomon, age ten, as an apprentice to a New York City cabinet- and chair maker. According to Philadelphia land records, in 1696, Maria bought property in Philadelphia. Between 1684 and 1700, Solomon moved to Philadelphia, joined the Society of Friends (Quakers), purchased land from his mother, and built a chairmaking shop. Over the course of his life, Cresson assimilated into the dominant Anglo culture, yet he continued to produce chairs that carried stylistic markers of his family's heritage.

Assimilated design ideas from a variety of sources are evident in this leather armchair with walnut frame (fig. 5). Essentially an English form, its molded uprights and arms with volute hand grips reflect Boston style. The sequence of turnings on the arm supports, consisting of a baluster with collar and incised line at its waist above a squat vase, reprises Philadelphia design. The leather-upholstered back extends into the half-round crest, which is embellished with moldings made with a transit, or "sweep." Consisting of an arm fitted with a shaped scraper at one end and point at the other, the sweep's point was anchored to the workpiece and the scraper swung back and forth in an arc, cutting the arched molding with each pass. The arched, molded crest and turned undercarriage of this chair relate to those of Swedish chairs such as an example at Winterthur Museum (fig. 6) that features a similar arched, molded crest and turning sequence of its stretchers. In his 1751 *Travels in America*, Swedish minister and botanist Peter Kalm commented on Swedish expatriates living in the Philadelphia area: "Before the English settled here, the colonists of New Sweden followed the customs of Old Sweden; but after the English had been in the country for some time, the Swedes began gradually to follow theirs [English customs]."

FIG. 6 *Side chair*, 1690–1720 | Beech, leather | 46⅝ x 18⅝ x 17⅝ in. | Delaware, New Jersey or Pennsylvania | Winterthur Museum, bequest of Henry Francis du Pont, 1954.0519

Chair makers introduced turned chairs with arched graduated slat backs to the Delaware Valley in the 1720s and continued to interpret the form into the next century. The design and configuration of the arched slats reflect a fusion of German and English traditions. Starting in the 1730s, Solomon Fussell (active 1726–c. 1750) updated the form by incorporating square-sawn "crookt feet" (cabriole legs) into frames assembled in the manner of traditional turned chairs using round tenons (fig. 7). He nailed nonstructural arched and scalloped boards to the sides and front of the seat frame purely for show, in emulation of more expensive joined chairs with scalloped seat rails. Invariably, the frames of chairs such as this example were painted black, brown, or red.

In 1952, Winterthur Museum curator Joseph Downs observed that "the foliation at the knees" of this armchair (fig. 8), the splat veneered with highly figured walnut, the concaved seat rail, and S-shaped spirals of the crest "are marks of the highest development of mid-eighteenth century colonial chair-making." In the late 1730s and early 1740s, Philadelphia chair makers began to produce compass-seat chairs that departed radically from what had come before. As furniture historian Allan Miller has noted, these new-style chairs "were the most avant-garde and conceptually evolved products of chairmaking shops." Inspired by Chinese chairs with ergonomically contoured backs, the S-shaped "crook'd back" or "India back" had come into fashion in London in the 1720s and was incorporated into the leather chairs with turned undercarriages that Boston chair makers produced in vast quantities for export to New York, Philadelphia, and the South. A decade later, chair makers incorporated "crook'd backs" into their new designs, echoing and harmonizing the ergonomic curves with other curved elements: vase-shaped splats joined to curved, continuous stiles and crests, either S-curve or hoop arms, compass seats, and cabriole legs. Production of these sinuous elements required mastery not only of shaping tools such as draw-knives and spokeshaves—edge tools especially adapted to shaping and smoothing rounded surfaces—but also of the design and layout of parts, taking into account extra material needed for the crest, leg, and seat rail carvings, and for clamping "ears" protruding from the upper ends of the arched stiles (used to clamp the back to the seat frame to stabilize the chair while shaping the stiles and executing the crest carving; these ears were sawn off with final finishing).

FIG. 8 *Armchair*, 1740–1750 | Walnut, hard pine, white pine | 42¼ x 27 x 22½ in. | Philadelphia, Pennsylvania | Winterthur Museum, gift of Henry Francis du Pont, 1960.1037

Where did this new style come from? Building on the work of Joe Kindig Jr. and David Stockwell, Miller observes that the compass-seat chair "was the product of a new workforce" of Irish immigrants who arrived in Philadelphia in the 1720s to escape astronomically high rents and several years of bad harvests in Ireland. Cabinet- and chair makers among this working-class group had learned the new style from their Irish masters, who developed a technique of lapping horizontal seat rails together and attaching the legs either with protruding pentagonal pins driven through pentagonal holes chiseled through the lap joints of the seat rails or by protruding dovetails keyed to the front edges of the rails. In both cases, the outside edges of the lapped rails and leg joints were veneered. Other furniture historians including Benno Forman and Désirée Caldwell have argued that the Irish learned the new compass-seat style—and these particular techniques for joining the legs to the horizontal seat frames—from refugee protestant German craftsmen who had migrated first to London, then to northern England, Ireland, New York, and Philadelphia by the early 1720s.

Like other Philadelphia examples, this chair is constructed with horizontal seat rails joined with mortises and tenons and drilled with holes to accept single round tenons protruding from the tops of the legs. Appearing neither in Irish nor German compass-seat chairs with horizontal rails, this wedged round-tenon joint appears to be a Philadelphia innovation, executed by chair makers using specialty "dowelling" and "chair" bits (purchased and used in pairs, the former to shape the tenon, the latter to excavate the mortise). Horizontal seat rails were well-adapted to accommodate compass-shaped slip seats. Separate molded edges for the slip seat are glued to the tops of the side rails of this example and are scarfed to a molding carved from the solid on the front rail (thereby eliminating the need for veneer on the front).

Where did this new style come from?

Hailed as "the greatest achievements of the form in pre-rococo Philadelphia."

FIG. 9 *Side chair*,
1750–1760 | Walnut,
white pine | 40¼ x 21 x
20¼ in. | Philadelphia,
Pennsylvania | Winterthur
Museum, gift of Henry
Francis du Pont,
1960.1036

Wealthy Philadelphia patrons commissioned compass-seat chairs with horizontal seat frames and solid splats through the late 1750s, as documented by an invoice for a set embellished with carved shell and volutes on the crest that chair maker James made for Captain Samuel Morris in 1759. Hailed as "the greatest achievements of the form in pre-rococo Philadelphia," a set of compass-seat side chairs with arched, pierced splats, including this example (fig. 9), bridges the rococo taste that gained fashion in the 1760s. It closely relates to (and may be from the same set as) an example at the Philadelphia Museum of Art originally made for the 1760 marriage of Richard Waln (son of Nicholas Waln and Mary Shoemaker Waln) and Elizabeth Armitt, daughter of cabinetmaker and chair maker Joseph Armitt (who died in 1747). The rounded stiles above the seat and slip-seat moldings carved from solid seat rails indicate a date of manufacture in the 1750s. A carver (identified today by his carving on a high chest owned in the twentieth century by collector Francis P. Garvan) designed and executed the splat without reference to a published source. His splat design also graces a side chair and armchair with trapezoidal seats (figs. 10, 11), completing the transition to the rococo style.

FIG. 10 *Armchair,* 1715–1740 | Mahogany | 39¾ x 24 x 21¼ in. | Pennsylvania | Winterthur Museum, bequest of Henry Francis du Pont, 1959.1327

FIG. 11 *Armchair,* 1760–1775 | Mahogany, tulip poplar | 41⅜ x 28½ x 23½ in. | Philadelphia, Pennsylvania | Winterthur Museum, gift of Henry Francis du Pont, 1957.504

English immigrant carver John Pollard (1740–1787) and other workers in the shop of cabinetmaker Benjamin Randolph (1721–1791) probably made this chair (fig. 12) around the year 1775 for Philadelphia resident Isaac Cooper. In the early 1760s Randolph hired Pollard and fellow English émigré carver Hercules Courtenay (c. 1740–1784) to design and execute his most important commissions for carved architectural woodwork and furniture. After Courtenay established an independent carving shop in 1769, Pollard continued as Randolph's lead carver until forming a partnership with John Butts in 1773. His hand can be seen particularly in the distinctive pendant bellflowers carved on the crest rail and cabochons on the ears. Although Philadelphia tradesmen, including Randolph, participated in protests against British colonial tax policies in the 1760s and Philadelphia served as the political and financial center for the resistance leadership during the American Revolution, the dominant taste in architecture and furnishings had turned avowedly English by mid-century. Even the more elaborately carved examples of Philadelphia chairs such as this example conformed to an eighteenth-century Anglo aesthetic referred to as "plain style" and "neat." Solid wood frames worked into graceful designs with clean lines and embellished with flowing, naturalistic carving contained within the overall composition characterized the best "plain-style" furniture. Adapted from a chair design that Thomas Chippendale illustrated in plate XVI of his *Gentleman and Cabinet Maker's Director* (3rd ed., 1762), the crest and splat of this chair flow together, carved to suggest interwoven bands. The lively interplay of negative and positive shapes established within the splat and between the splat and stiles lightens the chair and balances its mass. The unadorned rectilinear seat rails rest the eye, offering a respite from the curves of the legs, arms, and back. Randolph and Pollard inflected their interpretation of Chippendale's design with an unmistakable Philadelphia accent, most notably the chair's wide stance, seat rails joined to the rear stiles with through-tenons, and muscular cabriole legs ending in ball-and-claw feet carved with robust vertical talons. Philadelphia cabinetmakers continued to design furniture with ball-and-claw feet long after the style had fallen out of fashion in England.

FIG. 12 *Armchair*, 1765–1780 | Mahogany, hard pine, tulip poplar, white cedar, brass | 38⅞ x 30¾ x 23½ in. | Philadelphia, Pennsylvania | Winterthur Museum, gift of Henry Francis du Pont, 1961.116

Furniture historians have celebrated seven surviving commode-seat side chairs, including this example (fig. 13) from an original set numbering as many as twenty, as American masterpieces "in the vanguard of the avant-garde," according to furniture historian Andrew Brunk. No other American chairs are known with saddle-shaped, or commode, seats. Recognized now as "the most stylistically advanced rococo furniture produced in colonial America," in their own day they were seen as extraordinary expressions of the taste, wealth, and status of their owners, John and Elizabeth (Lloyd) Cadwalader. Soon after their marriage in 1768, Philadelphia merchant John Cadwalader and Maryland plantation heiress Elizabeth Lloyd bought a Philadelphia town house and began extensive renovations. They commissioned Philadelphia's leading cabinetmakers, Benjamin Randolph and Thomas Affleck, to produce their best parlor furnishings, including this chair, approving a design that Randolph adapted from plate 15 of Thomas Chippendale's *Gentleman and Cabinet Maker's Director* (3rd ed., 1762), further modified with the addition of hairy-paw feet (which required greater skill to execute than ball-and-claw feet). From Thomas Affleck they commissioned additional furniture that master carvers James Reynolds and the partners Nicholas Bernard and Martin Jugiez carved en suite with the chairs. And they engaged English émigré upholsterer Plunkett Fleeson to upholster their seating furniture, including this chair.

The saddle shape of the seats, with upturned corners and serpentine half-upholstered rails, required a high degree of technical skill to execute. Fleeson charged the Cadwaladers for covering the chairs "over rail furnish'd in canvas," providing each with a neat foundation. He nailed webbing to the frame, pulling the front-to-back webbing very tight to define the curves, and he laid canvas on top, nailing it to the frame. He used curled animal-hair upholstery rolls wrapped in canvas to outline the edges of the sides and fronts, raising the seat edge half an inch in front and tapering to a quarter inch at the back of the sides. He stretched animal-hair pads in the shallow seat well, covered them with canvas nailed half-over the rails, keeping the canvas in tension to maintain the sweep of the curve. He separately billed the Cadwaladers for conforming slip covers of blue-and-white check, finished in matching fringe that followed the top of the carving.

Elizabeth enjoyed her opulently refitted home for six years before her death in 1776. That year, George Washington appointed John Cadwalader as brigadier-general of the Pennsylvania militia, and Cadwalader led the militia in the battles of Princeton, Trenton, Brandywine, Georgetown, and Monmouth. In 1778 he was offered, and declined, the post of brigadier-general of the Continental Army and returned to civilian life, serving in the Maryland legislature. In 1779, he married Willamina Bond. The couple lived in the Philadelphia house until 1785. John died the following year, while away from home.

Philadelphia was a leading center not only for innovation of high-style seating furniture but also for the introduction of less-expensive forms, particularly the Windsor chair. Philadelphia Windsor chairs influenced Windsor chair design and production throughout colonial North America. English civil servant Patrick Gordon may have brought the first Windsor chair to the colonies when he arrived in Philadelphia in 1726 to assume the post of lieutenant governor. By the 1740s, cabinet and chair makers such as David Chambers advertised in the *Pennsylvania Gazette* that they made Windsor chairs; and by the early 1750s, vessels loaded with Windsor chairs as speculative cargo were departing the Delaware River for the West Indies. Consisting of legs, armrests, and back components inserted directly into a plank seat, Windsor chairs required the labor and skills of a cabinetmaker to saw and shape the seat and crest, a turner to produce legs, stretchers, arm supports, and spindles, and a carver to carve arm terminals and crest volutes. As furniture historian Nancy Goyne Evans has noted, from the beginning, Philadelphia Windsor chair makers relied on interchangeable parts and stockpiles of prepared materials for quantity production.

This high-back Windsor with D-shaped seat (fig. 14) is marked with a brand "F. Trumble" for Philadelphia cabinetmaker Francis Trumble. Trumble adapted the English high-back Windsor chair design to local taste and practices, departing from English precedent most notably in his use of turned elements based on the turned designs used in the arm supports and stretchers of Delaware Valley slat-back chairs (see fig. 7). The identifying features of Philadelphia workmanship in this chair include ball feet, cylindrical turned passages on the legs to accommodate the stretcher, wide D-shaped seat, raking back, and arms that are higher in the front than back and supported on crisply turned elements with vase-like buds at their tops. The shaped crests of high-style rococo seating furniture and the carved volutes on the crests of late baroque chairs inspired

FIG. 14 *Windsor armchair*, 1755–1762 | Hickory, ash, tulip poplar, maple, silver, paint | 44⅞ x 26⅞ x 26¾ in. | Philadelphia, Pennsylvania | Winterthur Museum, museum purchase, 1978.106

the design of this chair's crest. To meet the needs of a booming export market, in 1775, Trumble advertised a stock of twelve hundred Windsor chairs and solicited country craftsmen to supply forty thousand hand-shaved spindles, suggesting that he contracted with sawyers, turners, and carvers to mass-produce his designs. Windsor chair makers in New York City, Newport, Boston, and the Connecticut River Valley adapted Philadelphia style in their own designs.

Elite Philadelphians turned their drawing rooms into unofficial hubs for entertaining public officials—members of the so-called "Republican court"—foreign dignitaries, business and civic leaders and their wives and daughters.

PHILADELPHIA IN THE NEW REPUBLIC

During the American Revolution, many Philadelphia merchant families maintained trade contacts and lines of credit with their counterparts in England and the West Indies. After the war ended, they prospered, further developing trade with France and the Far East. In 1791, some of the city's wealthy financiers invested in the First Bank of the United States, helping to create what was, at the time, the largest corporation in America. As the seat of the fledgling federal government from 1790 to 1800, Philadelphia attracted many newcomers who had accepted government appointments or were seeking federal contracts. Cosmopolitan, prosperous, and civic-minded, the city's elites traveled abroad and welcomed foreign visitors to their city. Drawing-room entertaining became a central feature of the city's political and social life. Decorative arts historian Beatrice Garvan has noted that elite Philadelphians turned their drawing rooms into unofficial hubs for entertaining public officials—members of the so-called "Republican court"—foreign dignitaries, business and civic leaders and their wives and daughters. Many sought to appropriately furnish their parlors as congenial spaces for engaging guests in conversation about issues of the day, testing political opinions, discussing advances in science, the arts, and fashion, and displaying their taste, wit, and social skills. Wealthy and middling inhabitants alike were eager to commission furniture and decorations in the latest fashion. Chair styles that they deemed most appropriate for their new parlors and dining rooms followed designs adapted from George Hepplewhite's 1788 *Cabinetmaker and Upholsterer's Guide,* Thomas Sheraton's 1793 *Cabinet-Maker and Upholsterer's Drawing Book,* and *The Cabinet-Makers London Book of Prices,* first issued in Philadelphia in 1794. This work, the book most responsible for changing style in Philadelphia according to Garvan, listed prices for a variety of furniture forms and decorative options. Like the Philadelphia price book of 1772, it served both to standardize and stabilize labor costs across the highly competitive furniture-making industry and to inform cabinetmakers and consumers of the latest designs.

Whereas most Philadelphians looked to England for guidance in matters of taste, some, especially among the wealthy, began to take style cues from the French court. Residents appeared ambivalent about the unfolding French Revolution, finding their gratitude toward Louis XVI and members of the aristocracy for their support of the patriot cause during the American Revolution at odds with their sympathy for the insurgents seeking to overthrow the ancien régime. With little fanfare, French aristocrats such as Moreau de Saint-Méry and Charles Maurice de Tallyrand-Périgord, duc d'Orleans (future king of France, listed in the 1798 city directory simply as a merchant on Fourth Street), as well as royalist merchants and craftsmen, sought political asylum in Philadelphia during the height of violence, bringing with them furniture that caught the eye of their American cohorts. Their arrival, coupled with ongoing news of the Haitian and French Revolutions, generated interest in French neoclassical designs, and forms new to American consumers, such as bergères—low-back upholstered armchairs—started to appear in well-appointed drawing rooms. By 1811, Benjamin Henry Latrobe, an early proponent of French neoclassical architecture, articulated his optimism for the city in an address before members of the Society of Artists of the United States, a group he had recently helped to form. He hoped that "the days of Greece may be revived in the woods of America, and Philadelphia become the Athens of the Western world." And what more appropriate a style for this new Athens than a retrofitting of ancient Athenian designs? After the War of 1812, the French-inflected "empire" and "Greek Revival" styles gained widespread popularity.

Just as before the American Revolution, many Philadelphians continued to follow English fashion trends for their best parlor seating furniture in the era of the new republic. Every decorative option was available in the new taste: shield, oval, square backs; slip-seats and seats upholstered over-the-rails; straight, serpentine, and compass seats; straight-sided, turned, carved, inlaid, molded, and fluted legs—with and without stretchers; flared, turned, and spade feet. For chairs such as that in fig. 15, the chair maker adapted a design included in plate 7 of Hepplewhite's 1788 *Cabinet Maker and Upholsterer's Guide* in which a shield-shaped back with arched crest frames a pierced splat with strap-like elements emanating from a neatly carved pedestal and crossing in graceful arches at the top—a design made in large numbers in Philadelphia. Shield-shaped backs with rounded bottoms, called "urn-backs" in the 1796 *London Book of Prices*, were the most popular design in Philadelphia between 1790 and 1800; shield-shaped backs with pointed bottoms, designated "vase-backs," were less popular in Philadelphia than New York and New England. The serpentine front seat rail, side rails tenoned through the rear stiles, and tapered front legs molded with two beads and two hollows reflects the Philadelphia origin of this chair.

Before the American Revolution, few French immigrants had settled in Pennsylvania. Fleeing Catholic persecution after the revocation of the Edict of Nantes in 1685, a small number of protestant Huguenots from German-speaking towns along the Rhine assimilated into German communities surrounding Philadelphia. Between 1785 and 1825, however, two waves of French immigrants arrived in Philadelphia, bringing with them high-style Parisian furniture and craft skills and introducing French neoclassical designs to wealthy Philadelphians, setting a new standard of taste. As Beatrice Garvan has noted, the first wave, comprising aristocrats, royalists, merchants, cabinetmakers, upholsterers, and other craftsmen, immigrated after the onset of the French Revolution in 1789 and the second wave, including Napoléon's brother Joseph Bonaparte and his extensive retinue, arrived after Napoléon's defeat at the Battle of Waterloo in 1825. Carved, painted, gilded, and smartly upholstered armchairs of the type that the first wave of émigrés brought to Philadelphia had already attracted the attention of London designers George Hepplewhite (who called them "cabriole chairs") and Thomas Sheraton (who called them "drawing-room chairs"). Aware of this new taste, Thomas Jefferson, James Madison, and John Adams bought Parisian chairs while in France. Not to be

FIG. 15 *Side chair*, 1790–1800 | Mahogany, hard pine, tulip poplar | 38¾ x 21⅜ x 21 in. | Philadelphia, Pennsylvania | Winterthur Museum, bequest of Henry Francis du Pont, 1957.991

outdone, before moving from New York City to Philadelphia in 1790, George Washington bought several gilded French chairs from the French ambassador, Comte de Moustiers, sending one to a local chair maker to copy in order to fill out a set. By studying examples imported from France and illustrated in design books, English cabinetmakers learned the French styles. In 1787, William Long, an English-trained cabinetmaker living in Philadelphia, advertised his familiarity with French seating furniture, noting that he made "French Sophas in the modern taste ... Cabriole and French Chairs on reasonable terms ...." Likewise, the Paris-trained Philadelphia upholsterer Francis de L'Orme advertised "Cabriole and French chairs" and "Beds, Chairs, Arm-Chairs, and Couches, all in the English and French style."

Before moving from New York City to Philadelphia in 1790, George Washington bought several gilded French chairs from the French ambassador, Comte de Moustiers, sending one to a local chair maker to copy in order to fill out a set.

By tradition, this chair (fig. 16), one of a set that furniture historian Charles Montgomery hailed as "a monument to early American chairmaking," belonged to Robert Morris of Philadelphia. Embellished with carving, applied composition ornament, paint, and gilding, this chair features an upholstered back and open arms with upholstered pads and half-over-the-rails upholstered seat. Design elements that identify Philadelphia craftsmanship include the step-down arms; straight-tapered, reeded legs with drum-shaped elements at the top and turned spade feet; and the use of ash. The boxy, structured upholstery was achieved by a skilled upholsterer familiar with a technically complicated method requiring four stitching techniques. Quilting stitches with a straight needle secured animal-hair pads to the foundations. Diagonal stitches through the side wall and top panel with a curved needle stiffened the edges. Blind stitches with a straight needle through the side walls and top and returned

FIG. 16 *Armchair*, 1795–1805 | Ash | 36½ x 20½ x 21⅝ in. | Philadelphia, Pennsylvania | Winterthur Museum, Museum purchase with funds provided by the Special Fund for Collection Objects, 1991.66

through the same holes gathered the hair in loops and pulled it to the sides, stiffening and defining the side walls and preventing the hair from shifting. Multiple lines of diagonal stitches with a curved needle along the top edge of the side walls captured and compressed the hair into a stiff, sharp edge able to maintain its shape under repeated use.

At the forefront of designers who took neoclassicism in a new direction in the early nineteenth century, British-born American architect Benjamin Henry Latrobe (1764–1820) experimented with "classical historicism," designing buildings styled after Greek and Roman temples. In the belief that cohesive furnishings and interior decorations amplified the aesthetic power of his buildings, he designed furniture in what he called the "Etruscan" taste, which revived Greek and Roman forms, such as the klismos chair, for use in coordinated room settings. In 1805, the wealthy Philadelphia China merchant William Waln and his wife, Mary Wilcocks Waln, commissioned Latrobe to design and build their Philadelphia town house. In 1808, as the house neared completion, the couple requested that Latrobe furnish and decorate the principal rooms. His design for the drawing room called for a suite of painted tulipwood and maple furniture (including a pier table, a set of card tables, a set of chairs numbering between fifteen and twenty, two sofas, and two window benches) compatible in design, color, and decoration with a wall frieze "in flat Etruscan color" featuring black line-drawn adaptations of English artist John Flaxman's book illustrations for the *Odyssey* and *Iliad*. With saber legs and curved, severely rectilinear rails and tablet tops meant to evoke klismos chairs depicted on Greek pottery, the set of side chairs (fig. 17) dramatically departed from previous rococo and neoclassical forms. Latrobe may have found inspiration in the klismos-style chairs illustrated in European design books, such as those by English architect-designers Thomas Hope (*Household Furniture and Interior Decoration*, 1807) and George Smith (*A Collection of Designs for Household Furniture and Interior Decoration*, 1808).

FIG. 17 Designed by Benjamin Henry Latrobe | *Side chair,* 1808 | Oak, yellow poplar, white pine, plaster composition material; painted and gilded decoration; caning | 34¼ x 19½ x 22 in. | Philadelphia, Pennsylvania | Philadelphia Museum of Art, gift of Marie Josephine Rozet and Rebecca Mandeville Rozet Hunt, 1935.13.9

Although the pier table bears the signature of Philadelphia cabinetmaker and carpenter Thomas Wetherill, furniture historian Alexandra Kirtley has postulated that Wetherill possibly worked under the direction of Joseph Barry, whose firm, Joseph Barry & Son, Latrobe may have contracted to supply the suite to his designs. Born in Dublin, Joseph Barry was working in Philadelphia by the early 1790s in partnership with other cabinetmakers (including Lewis G. Affleck, son of cabinetmaker Thomas Affleck) before establishing his own shop in 1795. That year, he advertised furniture in the "newest London and French patterns," and his business thrived. Latrobe hired the talented British-born ornamental painter George Bridport to create the murals and hand paint-decorate the furniture. Each of the fifteen known chairs from the Waln set are painted with slightly different motifs. Evidence for the modern yellow silk drapery swags (of conjectural design) under the seat rails of this example (fig. 17) is based on fragments of original upholstery fabric found beneath the gesso and gilt decoration on the rails. This set may represent the earliest documented klismos-style chairs made in America.

The severe lines of this chair (fig. 18) are lightened and enlivened with die-cut brass inlay, influenced by French designs and referred to as "Boulle-work," after a decorative technique of tortoiseshell veneer inlaid with precious metal that André-Charles Boulle (1642–1732) innovated for furniture made for the court of Louis XV. In the early nineteenth century, English cabinetmaker George Bullock (1777–1818) revived the technique to great acclaim. During a visit to Liverpool in 1811, Philadelphia cabinetmaker Joseph Barry probably encountered and studied Bullock's work in Bullock's Liverpool showroom. After he returned to Philadelphia, he adapted the technique for his finest furniture, announcing in the September 11, 1824, issue of Philadelphia's *American Daily Advertiser* "2 Rich Sideboards, Buhl [Boulle] work and richly carved." Furniture scholar Page Talbott has discovered bills of sale and bills of lading for other Boulle-work furniture produced in his shop, further supporting the attribution.

Born in Dublin and trained there and in London, Joseph Barry immigrated to Philadelphia and is first listed in the city directory in 1794 as a cabinetmaker with business partner Alexander Calder. By 1797 the partnership had dissolved and he continued in his own shop, appearing regularly in city directories until 1833.

FIG. 18 *Side chair,* 1810–1820 | Mahogany veneer, rosewood veneer, brass, ebony, ash, white pine | 32 x 19 x 32¼ in. | Philadelphia, Pennsylvania | Winterthur Museum, museum purchase, 1988.35.2

Wealthy Philadelphia merchant George Harrison (1761–1845) acquired these chairs (fig. 19) from a Philadelphia cabinetmaker before 1830 and bequeathed them to his nephew, Joshua Francis Fisher, in whose family they descended until 1964. Their design, featuring distinctive dolphin arm supports, might have been inspired by chairs illustrated in English designer James Barron's *1813 Modern and Elegant Designs of Cabinet and Upholstery Furniture.* Tentatively attributed to Henry Connelly based on similarly posed dolphins with spade-like tail fins carved in the pedestals of a pair of card tables that Philadelphia merchant and financier Stephen Girard commissioned from Connelly in 1817, any of Philadelphia's leading cabinetmakers, including Anthony Quervelle, Michel Bouvier, and Joseph Barry, could have made them. In the 1820s, Anthony Quervelle used a label depicting a fanciful dressing table topped with supports in the shape of spouting dolphins to mark his work. Spouting dolphins became a familiar motif on English and American furniture after the War of 1812, popularized by large versions that London cabinetmaker William Collins included in his 1813 design for furniture memorializing the naval victories of Lord Horatio Nelson, commissioned by John Fish and given to the governor of Greenwich Hospital.

After his apprenticeship, Henry Connelly (1770–1826) was one of six cabinetmakers who opened shops in Newville, Pennsylvania, founded in 1790. He relocated to Philadelphia in 1799 where he employed at least one journeyman cabinetmaker, Robert McGuffin, and continued to work until his death in 1826.

INDUSTRIAL PHILADELPHIA

One of the busiest ports in the country, Philadelphia continued to grow after the federal government moved to Washington, DC, in 1800. That year, federal census-takers counted a population of 67,787 within the city limits and contiguous suburbs. Between 1815 and 1825, steam mills and the emergence of wholesale trade had begun to transform manufacturing. As throughout the city's history, foreign-born craftsmen continued to arrive in the city and cabinetmakers such as Anthony Quervelle, Michel Bouvier, and Alphonse LeJambre from France, and Adolphus Hoehling, David and George Klauder, Michael Deginter, Daniel Pabst, Gottlieb Vollmer, and Ferdinand Reazler from Germany entered the furniture business, establishing shops with specialized workforces, and furniture warerooms offering full lines of furniture and textiles and comprehensive design services. By 1850, 1,545 craftsmen worked in the furniture trades; thirty years later, in 1880, that number had more than doubled to 3,698. They manufactured furniture for export, executed large private commissions throughout the region, and served an urban population that had swelled to 565,529 by 1860 and 817,000 by 1876.

Marked "XII" on its seat rail, this chair (fig. 20) was one of an original set of at least twelve probably made for George and Mary K. Brinton of Birmingham Township, near present-day West Chester, under the direction of Philadelphia cabinetmaker Crawford Riddell. In its proportions and leg design it directly relates to gothic side chairs that Whig supporters of Henry Clay commissioned from the Society of Journeymen Cabinetmakers Ware-House (of which Riddell was superintendant) in 1844, as part of a suite of bedroom furniture for the White House in anticipation of Clay's victory in the 1844 presidential election. After his defeat, Clay sold the set to cotton planter Daniel Turnbull, who shipped the set to his Louisiana plantation, Rosedown. The design for this chair was adapted from plate 143 of English designer George Smith's *The Cabinet-Maker and Upholsterer's Guide* (London, 1826).

Crawford Riddell was first listed as a cabinetmaker in the 1835 Philadelphia directory. Between 1837 and 1844 he served as superintendent of the Society of Journeymen Cabinetmakers, overseeing the society's furniture warerooms, which, he announced in an advertisement in the 1839 Philadelphia city directory, carried "the largest assortment of Furniture of the latest and most approved designs to be found in any establishment in the United States all manufactured by the best Journeyman in the trade." Other Philadelphia chair makers such as Charles White and Abraham McDonough were probably producing variants of gothic side chairs, including models with both convex and concave crests, and it is possible that Riddell retailed their work. Between 1844 and 1849, Riddell operated his own wareroom, and in the July 17, 1845, issue of the New Orleans *Times Picayune* was included in a list of "Philadelphia Wholesale Houses" as a "Manufacturer of Splendid Cabinet Furniture and Ornamental Upholstery." In 1850, while aboard a steamer bound for California via the Cape Horn, he contracted a fatal case of cholera and was buried at sea.

FIG. 20 *Side chair*, 1840–1849 | Swietenia wood | 33 x 17½ x 20 in. | Philadelphia, Pennsylvania | Winterthur Museum, Museum purchase with funds provided by the Special Fund for Collection Objects, 1993.66.1

Known for furniture such as this upholstered parlor chair richly carved in the rococo revival style (fig. 21), George J. Henkels (1819–1883) was considered Philadelphia's leading furniture manufacturer in the mid-nineteenth century. Of German descent, Henkels was born in Philadelphia, apprenticed to a chair maker, and first listed in the city directory as a chair maker in 1843. He may have developed an association with Crawford Riddell; after Riddell's death in 1850, he moved into his premises and succeeded him in the furniture trade.

Historian Kenneth Ames observed that Henkels played a major role in introducing the rococo revival style in America. In the 1850s, Henkels capitalized on public demand for furniture in French revival styles by directly importing Parisian examples to copy and sell. He raised the cachet of his own wares by intermixing these imports with shop-made adaptations in his showroom, making it difficult for customers—and collectors today—to tell the difference between the two. And he adapted designs that French taste-maker Désiré Guilmard serially published in *Le Garde-meuble, ancien et moderne*, a periodical that Guilmard founded in 1839 (and that persisted until 1935). In 1850, soon after he took over Riddell's shop, he published for free distribution to customers *An Essay on Household Furniture*, illustrated with images of French furniture exhibited at the 1844 Paris Exposition of Industry and first published by Guilmard. He became friends with Samuel Sloan, a Philadelphia housebuilder, architect, and author of popular home design books, convincing Sloan to feature his furniture in his 1861 *Sloan's Homestead Architecture Containing Forty Designs for Villas, Cottages and Farm Houses*. Through high-quality products, savvy marketing, and self-promotion, Henkels parlayed his business into one of the city's largest warerooms after the Civil War. He died a widower at age sixty-four, in 1883, leaving thirteen children.

He raised the cachet of his own wares by intermixing these imports with shop-made adaptations in his showroom, making it difficult for customers— and collectors today—to tell the difference between the two.

This upholstered parlor chair (fig. 22) is attributed to Allen and Brother based on furniture that the firm made combining Renaissance, Egyptian, neo-Grec, and "Assyrian" revival styles.

Philadelphia furniture maker and fancy goods dealer William Allen Sr. (d. 1869) established a shop in 1835. He trained his sons Joseph (b. 1818) and William Allen Jr. (d. 1865) in the trade and brought them into the business, which he had expanded to include trade in exotic tropical hardwoods. In 1847, his sons took over the company. Four years after William's death, in 1869, Joseph entered into partnership with his brother James C. Allen (b. 1825) and, operating under the name "Allen & Brother," they solidified a reputation for fine cabinetwork. Rivaling George Henkels's manufactory and warerooms, Allen & Brother became one of Philadelphia's largest makers of Victorian furniture, as furniture historian Page Talbott has observed. Lauding the company in his 1875 survey *The Manufactories and Manufacturers of Pennsylvania of the Nineteenth Century*, Charles Robson observed: "All the work [by the Allens] is hand-made and of the most elaborate designs, no machinery being used ... The most skilled workmen to be obtained in Europe or America are employed, and they are of various nationalities. Their work is strictly of the custom class and they have but one price—that decided upon in their first estimate. Their reputation was founded by their superior work, and they never undertake to do 'cheap' work, or, in other words, inferior—work. Their workmen are of the most skilled and best paid, and in busy times they employ about 115 in the various departments of their manufactures."

Allen and Brother continued to 1896, when James C. took over, assisted by Joseph A. Allen Jr. James closed the firm in 1902.

Daniel Pabst (1826–1910) probably made this chair (fig. 23) for the boardroom of the Pennsylvania Academy of Fine Arts, following a design by Philadelphia architect Frank Furness (1839–1912), who, with his partner, George Hewitt, designed and built the academy's new headquarters between 1871 and 1876. Pabst and Furness worked within the Renaissance revival and reformed gothic styles touted by English designers such as Bruce J. Talbert (*Gothic Forms Applied to Furniture, Metalwork, and Decoration for Domestic Purposes*, London, 1867, Boston, 1873), Christopher Dresser (*Principles of Decorative Design*, London, 1873), and Charles Lock Eastlake (*Hints on Household Taste*, London, 1868).

FIG. 22 Attributed to Allen and Brother | *Side chair*, 1865–1875 | Walnut with ebonized decoration | 45 x 25 x 25 in. | Philadelphia, Pennsylvania | Philadelphia Museum of Art: Gift of Federick LaValley and John N. Whitenight, 2010.20.1

FIG. 23 Designed by
Frank Furness. Possibly
made by Daniel Pabst |
Side chair, 1870–1871 |
Walnut, ash, bald
cypress; modern leather
upholstery | 30¾ x 17¼ x
24 in. | Philadelphia,
Pennsylvania |
Philadelphia Museum of
Art: Gift of George Wood
Furness, 1974.224.2

Counted among the foremost cabinetmakers working in Philadelphia after the Civil War, Pabst was born in Langenstein, Hesse-Darmstadt, Germany, and trained as a cabinetmaker at a local trade school. He immigrated to Philadelphia in 1849. He quickly found work as a journeyman cabinetmaker, and within five years, in 1854, opened his own shop. He formed a partnership with German émigré cabinetmaker Frank Krauss, and was listed in the 1866 city directory as "Pabst and Krauss." By 1870, he had assumed sole proprietorship of the firm and employed as many as fifty journeymen. He established a working relationship with architect Frank Furness, contracting furniture and interior woodwork on many Furness commissions, including the 1873 overhaul of Theodore Roosevelt Sr.'s New York town house. Pabst also executed contracts from Furness's competitors, such as Philadelphia architects Collins and Autenrieth, and he designed, manufactured, and marketed furniture of his own design, winning a medal of excellence at the 1876 Philadelphia Centennial for a monumental sideboard. The authors of the Pennsylvania Historical Review's 1886 guide *City of Philadelphia: Leading Merchants and Manufacturers* described Pabst as "Designer and Manufacturer of Artistic Furniture," noting that he "designs and manufactures art and antique furniture of all kinds, which, for beauty and originality of design, superior and elaborate finish are unexcelled. The trade of the house extends through this and adjacent States." He retired in 1896 at age seventy and died in 1910.

RISE OF CRAFT STUDIOS

As national manufacturing companies took over the design, production, and mass-marketing of home furnishings by the end of the nineteenth century, some Philadelphia artisans worked individually or in small group studios to create furniture that reflected tenets of the English arts and crafts movement. They emphasized high-quality materials such as solid native hardwoods and hand-worked iron, primacy of functionality in their designs, and simplicity of decoration, incorporating joinery as an important aesthetic element. Some referenced medieval and gothic styles in their work. Furniture historians David Barquist and Elizabeth Agro have noted that several key Philadelphia educational institutions founded in the nineteenth century not only provided practical training in design and methods but also helped to create the intellectual and cultural climate in which these artisans framed their enterprises. These included the Pennsylvania Academy of the Fine Arts (1805); Philadelphia School of Design for Women (1848); Pennsylvania Museum and School of Industrial Art (1876); Philadelphia Textile School (1884); Drexel Institute of Art, Science, and Industry (1891); and the Graphic Sketch Club (1898). At the turn of the twentieth century, craft-based communities began to appear in Philadelphia's exurbs. Sculptor Frank Stephens and architect William Lightfoot Price founded the utopian community of Arden, Delaware, complete with craft shops in which furniture was produced, and, in 1901, Price established the arts and crafts community of Rose Valley, near Media, Pennsylvania, with furniture and ceramics workshops. In this period, artists, some of whom trained at the Pennsylvania Academy of Fine Arts, began to settle along the banks of the Delaware River in the vicinity of New Hope, Pennsylvania, approximately forty miles north of Philadelphia. Within a decade, the town had acquired a reputation as an arts colony and began to attract artisans and furniture makers.

This folding chair (fig. 24), modeled directly on a Tyrolean *faltstuhl* from the late fifteenth or early sixteenth century, reflects the historicist aesthetic and "structural idea" of its designer, William Lightfoot Price (1861–1916), wherein the chair's structure is reflected in its construction. Following Price's design, workmen in the woodworking shop of Rose Valley, a community based on arts and crafts principles that Price and others founded in 1901 near Media, Pennsylvania, crafted and carved it by hand from machine-milled and -planed stock.

Born into a Quaker family, William Lightfoot Price attended the Quaker Westtown School, leaving in 1877 to practice carpentry. At age seventeen, he sought training as an architect, first in the Philadelphia offices of Addison Hutton, then with Frank Furness. With his brother, Francis Price, he opened a practice in 1881, continuing in the partnership until 1895. In 1903, he formed a partnership with M. Hawley McClanahan that lasted until his death. Interested in social reform, he joined with sculptor Frank Stephens to found the utopian arts and crafts community Arden, near Wilmington, Delaware, in 1900, based on Henry George's single-tax theory. A year later, he founded Rose Valley, a community based on the writings of John Ruskin and William Morris, devoted to the "manufacture of ... materials and products involving artistic handicraft as are used in the finishing, decorating and furnishing of houses," according to the act of incorporation. At Rose Valley, he adapted William Morris's idea of the "banded workshop" in which artisans working in a variety of media shared

FIG. 24 William L. Price | *Chair*, c. 1901–1909 | Oak | 29 x 23½ x 24¾ in. | Moylan, Pennsylvania |
Philadelphia Museum of Art: Purchased with the Thomas Skelton Harrison Fund, 1995.52.1

facilities. In 1902, he appointed Belgian émigré woodworker and carver John Maene (1863–1928) as foreman of the furniture shop. Having trained in woodworking and carving in their native Belgium, John and his uncle, Edward Maene, settled in Philadelphia in 1880. By 1894 they had established a workshop and John advertised his skills as a sculptor capable of making "art furniture." After Rose Valley's workshops closed in 1906, John and Edward continued to make furniture in the modern gothic, revival, and arts and crafts styles through the 1920s.

WHARTON ESHERICK (1887-1920)

To create the curved rear feet and half-round front leg/arm elements of his iconic "Wagon Wheel Chair" (fig. 25), Wharton Esherick deployed a method traditionally used to produce the hoop-shape backs of sack-back Windsor chairs: steam bending tree-wet wood. The resulting arc of the front leg/arm components alludes to the sawn wooden felloes of the wheels on the ubiquitous haywagons and barnyard carts of his Paoli, Pennsylvania, neighbors' farms. The support strut of the cantilevered seat playfully evokes the idea of spokes. Much like a snowshoe, the back and seat are fashioned from woven strips of leather looped around the frame—a lightweight material with enough "give" to comfortably accommodate the sitter. Although this minimalist design radically departed from the neo-medieval furniture that William Lightfoot Price produced a generation before in the nearby Rose Valley workshops, it expressed the arts and crafts ethos of revealing joinery, evident here in the exposed through-tenons of the struts and seat rails on the backs of the rear legs. In this chair's design, Esherick brought to bear Austrian philosopher Rudolph Steiner's ideas about organic functionalism in which an object's design is determined by its intended use and its aesthetic relationship to associated objects and spaces.

Born in Philadelphia to a prosperous merchant family, Esherick learned wood- and metalworking at the Manual Training High School, after which he studied drawing and printmaking at the Pennsylvania Museum School of Industrial Art and painting at the Pennsylvania Academy of Fine Arts. In 1913, he and his wife, Letty Hofer, moved to a small farm in Paoli, Pennsylvania, and set up a studio where he worked in a variety of media, including wood, producing two-dimensional works and sculpture. Both became immersed in the progressive intellectual, artistic, and cultural life of the Rose Valley community, especially its Hedgerow Theatre for which Esherick designed and built stage sets, experimenting with

FIG. 25 Wharton Esherick | *Wagon Wheel Chair*, 1931 | Hickory, laced leather seat and back | 39¾ x 20 x 22 in. | Paoli, Pennsylvania | Wharton Esherick Museum Collection | Mark Sfirri and the Wharton Esherick Museum

expressionism, futurism, and cubism. In 1927, discouraged by New York gallery owners' lack of interest in his paintings, he put down his paintbrushes for good and concentrated on wood sculpture, furniture, and utensils in a style stripped of what he called "literature"—ornate surface decoration that distracted attention from their essential forms and vitiated their sculptural power. By 1928, with the help of assistant John Schmidt (who would continue to work with him for the next thirty years) he made innovative wooden furniture inspired by European modernism—"expressionist" designs with hard-edge asymmetric, geometric shapes and components—and sold his works to friends and acquaintances by word of mouth. Over the next several decades, he transformed his house and studio into an artistic living and work space in which he could conduct design experiments and show his work. With the exception of a bandsaw that he made using bicycle components in the 1960s, throughout his career (and with the continuing help of Schmidt and other occasional assistants) he used only hand tools and methods. In the mid-1940s he developed a softer-edge style, relying on organic forms that came to define his later work. After World War II, a new generation of craftsmen found inspiration in his furniture and, in 1958–1959, the Museum of Contemporary Crafts in New York City hosted a retrospective exhibition. Many credit him with breathing new life into the studio furniture movement and defining twentieth-century style in American craft furniture.

GEORGE NAKASHIMA (1905-1990)

Nakashima created this chair (fig. 26) early in his career as a full-time studio furniture maker in New Hope, Pennsylvania. Many of its characteristics, such as the open design utilizing unadorned tapered turned elements, the juxtaposed angles of the legs, seat, spindles and crest, crest and seat with tapered profiles, and rush seat with extended weft elements worked through holes drilled in the seat rails (a construction technique designed as decorative element), are hallmarks of his later work. Like William Lightfoot Price's arts and crafts furniture made at Rose Valley and Wharton Esherick's furniture, the joinery is visible as an "honest" merging of form and function, a key component of the mid-century modern aesthetic. In his 1981 book, *The Soul of a Tree: A Woodworker's Reflections*, Nakashima avowed that "for the sake of honesty," he used only solid, plain-sawn wood in all of his work. Open about his use of industrial-grade machine tools in conjunction with hand work, he nonetheless prided himself on his meticulous attention to detail in all of his commissions, designing and hand-crafting furniture in the early 1940s at a time when, as he later recollected, "crafts-manship was not regarded as an important concept."

Born in Spokane, Washington, George Nakashima received a bachelor's degree in architecture from the University of Washington in 1929 and a master's degree in architecture from the Massachusetts Institute of Technology in 1930. He traveled to Tokyo where he worked for the American architect Antonin Raymond, spending two years overseeing a construction project in India. After returning to the United States in 1941, he married and moved back to Seattle, finding work with Seattle-based architect Ray Morin. In his spare time, he made furniture of his own design in the basement of the Maryknoll Boy's Club in exchange for teaching woodworking to the young men served by the charity. During World War II, the US government relocated him and his family to Camp Minidoka, a Japanese internment camp in Hunt, Idaho. There, he met woodworker Gentauro Hikogama, from whom he learned traditional Japanese carpentry techniques. Sponsored by Antonin Raymond, he was released from Camp Minidoka and he moved to Raymond's farm in New Hope, Pennsylvania. In 1946, he established a nearby craft-furniture studio and shop where he designed and built furniture on commission and for two commercial lines he created for Knoll and Widdicomb-Mueller.

PHILLIP LLOYD POWELL (1919–2008)

Known for furniture with sinuous lines and deep-carved work following the wood figure and emphasizing irregularities, Phillip Lloyd Powell designed this chair (fig. 27) following European modernist principles. He chose walnut, finding the wood well-suited to shaping with a spokeshave and other edge tools needed to create curved surfaces.

Born August 26, 1919, in Germantown, Pennsylvania, Phillip Lloyd Powell began making furniture as a teenager. He studied mechanical engineering at Drexel Institute of Technology before being drafted to serve in World War II as an Army Air Corps weather forecaster in Britain. After the war, in 1947, he bought an acre of land in New Hope, Pennsylvania, bought a book on house building, and constructed his home. He befriended George Nakashima, who lived nearby, and began to restore antiques and build furniture inspired by Wharton Esherick's and Nakashima's designs, primarily from rejected wood (much of it gleaned from Nakashima's workshop). After completing a contract from Macy's Department

FIG. 27 Phillip Lloyd Powell | *Lounge Chairs,* 1960 | Walnut, leather | 30 x 12 x 28½ in. | Galere

FIG. 28 Paul Evans | *Patchwork Dining Chair*, 1970 | Blackened welded steel, patinated copper, bronze, and pewter, parchment leather seats | 34 x 28 x 26 in. | New Hope, Pennsylvania | Todd Merrill Studio

Store for one thousand child's footstools, he swore off commissions requiring mass production. In 1953, he refurbished a storefront in New Hope from which, one night a week, he sold Herman Miller furniture, Isamu Noguchi lamps, rebuilt antiques, and furniture of his own design. Soon thereafter, he partnered with Paul Evans, sharing studio and showroom space and collaborating on furniture and accessories. Powell later reflected on this association: "Paul helped me refine my engineering-based designs, as his background was in the arts—and in return I turned his art into furniture." In 1961, Powell and Evans exhibited their works in a two-man show at America House in New York, leading to a commission from Directional, a furniture company that sponsored young designers. Dissatisfied with corporate culture, temperamentally suited to designing unique objects for individual clients, Powell broke with Evans in 1964. Working alone and with occasional assistants, Powell produced approximately one thousand pieces of furniture over the course of his career, choosing to spend income earned on individual commissions traveling the globe.

PAUL EVANS (1931-1987)

Born May 20, 1931, in Trenton, New Jersey, Paul Evans's artistic abilities caught the eye of philanthropist Aileen Vanderbilt Webb, who helped him secure a scholarship to Cranbrook Academy. There, Evans studied metalwork, silver- and goldsmithing, sculpture, and jewelry. Months before completing his degree, he moved to Old Sturbridge Village in Massachusetts (also partially supported by Aileen Vanderbilt Webb) to work as a "living history" craftsman, demonstrating colonial silversmithing techniques. In 1951, he decided to reenroll at a different art school, the School for American Craftsmen in Rochester, New York. En route to Rochester, he passed through New Hope, Pennsylvania, and stopped at Phillip Lloyd Powell's shop. Powell and Evans immediately hit it off and, even though he was twelve years Powell's junior, Evans negotiated placing his works in Powell's showroom. Powell encouraged Evans to develop larger pieces and the two collaborated on joint works of walnut and steel. Both approached their materials in a similar way: Powell allowed the figure and irregularities of the wood to guide his carving and design, amplifying these features in his finished work; Evans accentuated evidence of metalworking techniques—rough, unfinished marks from the milling, forging, and welding processes—in the metal used to fabricate his furniture. In 1957 he exhibited his work as a participant in a Museum of Contemporary Craft exhibition, enlarging public interest in his designs. In 1959, he hired Dorsey Reading, a machinist from Lambertville, New Jersey, to execute his designs, some of which proved so toxic to produce that they had to be abandoned.

Evans's and Powell's work caught the attention of high-end Manhattan furniture supplier Bud Mesberg, who commissioned six tables for his influential shop, Directional. Then, in 1961, Powell and Evans mounted a two-man show at America House (partially funded by Aileen Vanderbilt Webb), which brought national attention to their work. In 1964, unwilling to scale up production, Powell broke off the partnership and, from 1964 to 1980, Evans oversaw large-scale production of his designs for Directional Furniture Company, opening a thirty-thousand-square-foot facility in Plumsteadville, Pennsylvania, in 1970. Between thirty-four and ninety workers produced between three hundred and four hundred pieces each week. In 1981, Evans ended his relationship with Directional and opened his own New York City showroom, displaying elaborate works with motorized components. By 1987, this endeavor failed and he retired. He died at his Nantucket home the day after he closed his New York showroom.

ROBERT WHITLEY (B. 1924)

Made from American curly maple, ebony, dogwood, bird's-eye maple, and black walnut, the design of this circa 1999 *Throne Chair* (fig. 29) evokes an eighteenth-century corner chair. Whitley fashioned it using an innovative technique he called "pillowing" in which the surface edges are joined in a way to allow for the expansion and contraction of the wood components in reaction to atmospheric moisture.

A third-generation woodworker and furniture conservator, New Hope, Pennsylvania–based studio furniture designer Robert Whitley was born in 1924. He attended Trenton Art School in Trenton, New Jersey, and embarked on a career restoring antiques and building furniture to his own designs, winning the 1966 National Merit Award from the Museum of Contemporary Crafts for his Starfish desk. In 1971 he and his wife purchased land in Solebury, Pennsylvania, where he established a shop. In addition to designing furniture, he has worked on important conservation commissions, including the 1978 reproduction for the John F. Kennedy Presidential Library of the intricately carved *Resolute* desk originally gifted to Rutherford B. Hayes by Queen Victoria in 1888 and used by John F. Kennedy in the Oval Office.

FIG. 29 Robert Whitley | *Throne Chair*, ca. 1999 | Curly maple, ebony, dogwood, American black walnut, bird's-eye maple | 34 x 34¾ x 27 in. | Bucks County, Pennsylvania | James A. Michener Art Museum. Gift of Steve and Suzanne Kalafer and Flemington Car and Truck Country, 2008.11.2

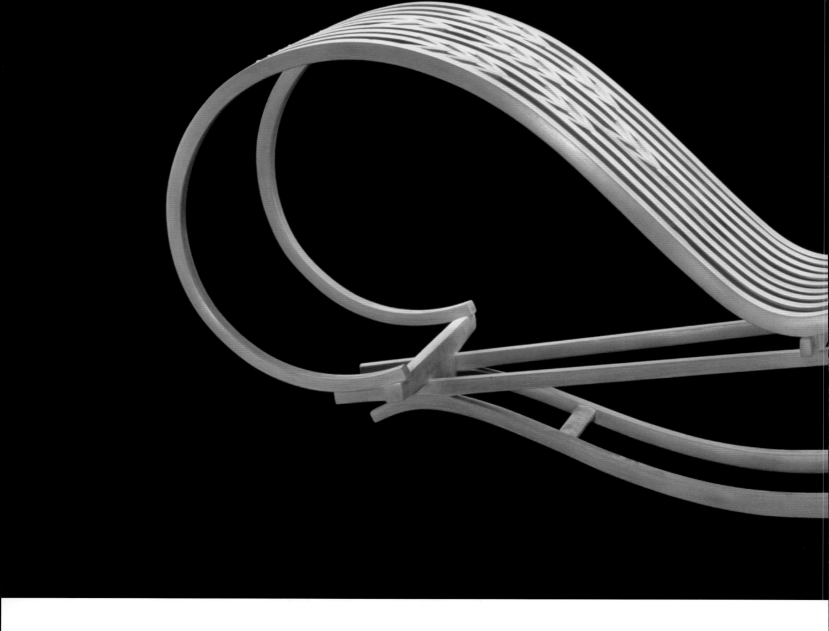

MICHAEL HURWITZ (B. 1955)

Born in Miami, Florida, in 1955, Michael Hurwitz was raised outside of Boston. In 1974–1975 he attended the Massachusetts College of Art in Boston, intent on learning how to make stringed instruments. He transferred to the Boston University Studio program and redirected his focus to furniture, graduating with a BFA in 1979. In 1985 he moved to Philadelphia to assume a teaching position

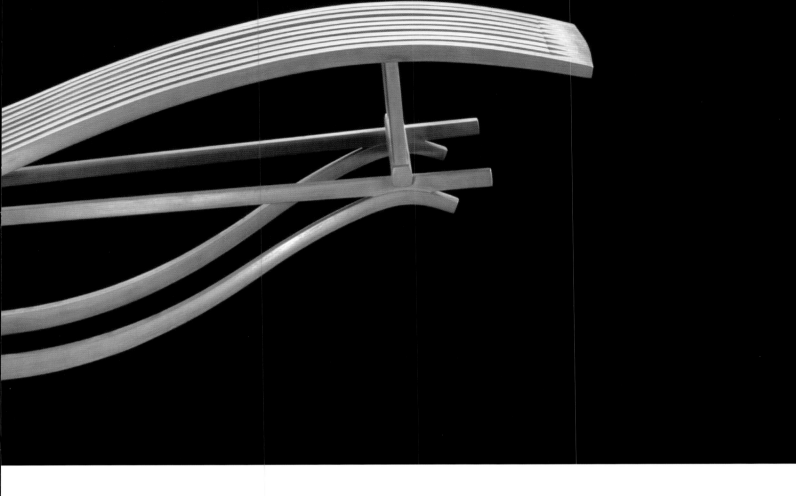

at the University of the Arts, serving as head of the wood department in 1989. That year, he was awarded a grant from the National Endowment for the Arts, enabling him to travel and study in Japan. On his return, he focused on his independent work as a designer and furniture craftsman, developing relationships with galleries across the United States. In 2014 he was inducted into the American Craft Council College of Fellows.

FIG. 30 Michael Hurwitz | *Rocking Chaise*, 1989 | Laminated mahogany, steel pipe, yellow ochre milk paint | 36 x 90 x 24 in. | Philadelphia, Pennsylvania | Gift of Anne and Ronald Abramson, the Renwick Alliance, museum purchase made possible by the Smithsonian Institution Collections Acquisition Program © Michael Hurwitz

KNOLL INDUSTRIES (EST. 1938)

Designed by Philadelphia native Robert Venturi and produced by Greenville, Pennsylvania–based firm Knoll, this cheeky postmodern take on rococo style (fig. 31) showcases modern materials and manufacturing techniques while referencing the past. One of nine different designs, each of which invokes a specific historical furniture style, this example riffs on a design popularized by English cabinetmaker Thomas Chippendale. It is included here to advance the story of innovative chair production in greater Philadelphia through its power to evoke Philadelphia's preeminent position as the leading center of cabinet- and chairmaking at the time of the American Revolution. Expressing an ironic populist sensibility, its cartoon-like, oversize silhouette featuring a gothic pierced splat, and its all-over plastic laminate surface printed with a banal, pastel floral pattern called "Grandmother's Tablecloth," plays on the florid naturalistic leafage carved on eighteenth-century Philadelphia's best rococo chairs. Its accessible, simplified design and decoration would appear to strip away the elitist associations of the form to which it alludes—even as it was marketed and priced to upscale consumers.

FIG. 31 Designed by Robert Venturi | *Chippendale Chair*, Designed 1978–1984, manufactured 1985 | Bent laminated wood; plastic laminate | 37½ x 23⅛ x 18½ in. | Knoll, East Greenville, Pennsylvania | Philadelphia Museum of Art: Gift of Collab: The Group for Modern and Contemporary Design at the Philadelphia Museum of Art, 1985.94.4

Expressing an ironic populist sensibility, its cartoon-like, oversize silhouette featuring a gothic pierced splat, and its all-over plastic laminate surface printed with a banal, pastel floral pattern called "Grandmother's Tablecloth," plays on the florid naturalistic leafage carved on 18th-century Philadelphia's best rococo chairs.

Hans Knoll (1914–1955) was born in Germany to a furniture-making family. His grandfather founded a cabinetmaking shop in 1865 and his father expanded and modernized the business, producing early Mies van der Rohe designs in his Stuttgart factory. In the late 1930s, Knoll immigrated to England and, in 1937, established a short-lived interior design company. In 1938, he moved to New York City and founded the Hans G. Knoll Furniture Company, pairing with furniture designer Jens Risom to produce a line of modern office furniture. In 1941 he retrofitted a former dance hall in East Greenville, Pennsylvania, as a furniture factory. The company prospered and, in 1943, Knoll hired architect and interior designer Florence Schust to expand the company's services to include commercial interior design, launching the Knoll Planning Unit under her direction in 1945. A year later, in 1946, Knoll and Schust married and changed the company name to Knoll Associates. Knoll offered to pay royalties for designs—a business innovation that enabled the company to attract the design services of international modernists such as Harry Bertoia, Eliel Saarinen, and Ludwig Mies van der Rohe. In 1950, Knoll relocated its headquarters to East Greenville, Pennsylvania. After Hans Knoll died in an automobile accident in 1955, Florence guided the company as president, serving in the post until 1960. From 1960 to her retirement in 1965, she oversaw the company's design and development departments. Knoll continues to operate today from its East Greenville headquarters.

Joshua Lane

The Lois F. and Henry S. McNeil Curator of Furniture,
Winterthur Museum, Garden & Library

Juror Essays

Slouching Toward the Apocalypse

Your chair is killing you. I am acutely aware of that as I sit down to write this. We have reached a point in civilization where so many of the things we crave and surround ourselves with have become our downfalls, and here we find another. As a species, we have never been good at moderation.

The truth is that we spend considerably more time sitting in chairs than thinking about them, and we probably shouldn't. Studies suggest that the average person in this country spends twelve hours each day sitting, which makes us the most sedentary generation in history. And this "sitting disease" contributes to a number of health issues, from chronic back problems and fatigue to rising rates of obesity, diabetes, and heart disease, which cannot be counteracted by an hour of exercise here and there.[1] Each day, we sit in our cars or on buses or subways as we commute to work. We arrive and assume the position at our desks, and at the end of the day, we return home, only to lounge in front of our televisions and personal computers. And that is perhaps why an exhibition such as this is most valuable. Here we have an opportunity to turn the tables, to think for a moment about the chair, with all of its ingenious, comfortable, complex, and, yes, insidious qualities.

The chair is a feat of engineering, as any craftsman would tell you, and it is a more difficult problem than it often receives credit for. How many of us walk into a dining room and admire the table, while the chair—the star!—hides demurely underneath? But here is an object with a strong sense of purpose. It must bear the weight of the largest man as he squirms in his seat and pushes back into its legs. Yet it must also accommodate a more delicate sitter, extending to him or her the same courtesy. For the craftsman, building a single chair, with all the effort it takes, must be a labor of love, since the best chair is often the one we forget we're sitting in. As Martin Eidelberg points out, "During the second half of the nineteenth century, the focus of attention was the sideboard or cabinet, because it offered a large expanse on which craftsmen could display their expertise in carving and inlay."[2] The craftsman received many more accolades for the sideboard. Thus it was not until the designer got involved that the chair achieved its status as icon.

The physical challenge is one reason the chair excited the designer, who delights in problem solving. But it is joined by several more: First, its white-collar ubiquity, its broad use in every home, office, and public space, makes it among the most visible designed elements in our environment.

Second, a broad array of production considerations come into play, each with its own unique design challenge, which make it a rich subject to explore. There is a need for a chair to suit every space, occasion, and budget, so there are infinite competing needs to fulfill. What room will my chair occupy? Who is its target audience, and how will they use it? Is it sustainable? Compact? Does it move around easily, or must it stay put? Is its production wasteful? Is it economical to ship? All good questions.

But perhaps most importantly, the chair is an idea. In its perfect scale and purpose, it makes natural reference to the figure, like a stand-in for the body itself. It is an intimate architecture built to house a single person, a doppelgänger for the designer who made it. And by virtue of that relationship, the chair goes further, literally, physically molding us into its own image, asking its sitter to adapt to its parameters. It punishes him if he is too tall, too short, too hunched, too fidgety, if any physical characteristic is out of order. As we sit, we acquiesce, handing over our power and conforming to its shape. These characteristics imbue it with powerful ideological potential. Every element reflects back squarely on us.

The chair is a feat of engineering, as any craftsman would tell you,

and it is a more difficult problem than it often receives credit for.

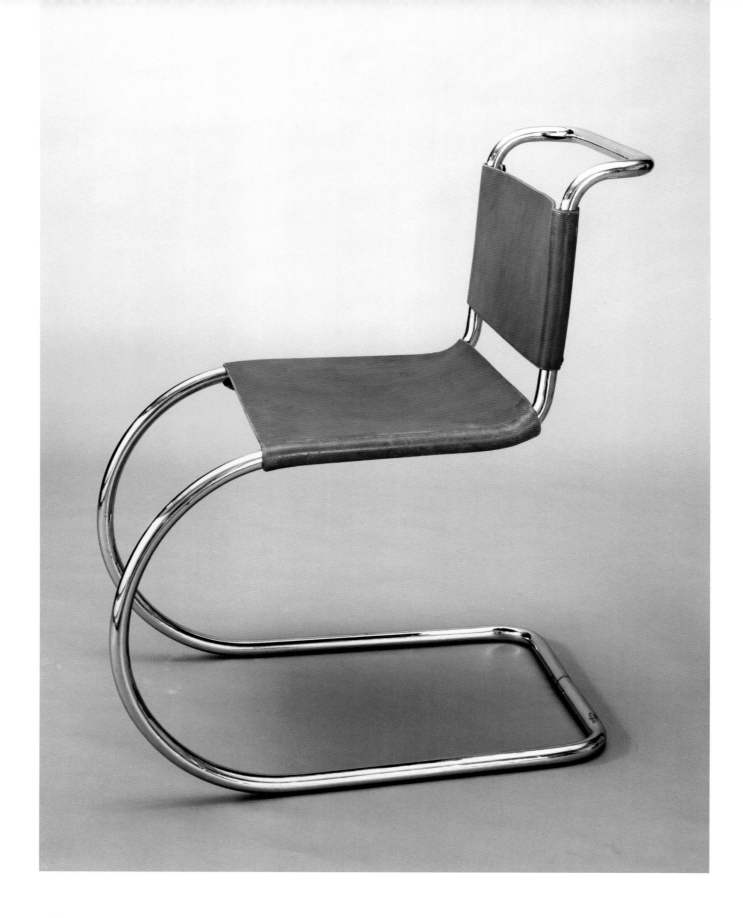

Ludwig Mies van der Rohe | *MR Side Chair*, 1927 | Chrome-plated steel tubing, leather | 31 x 18 ½ x 28 ⁵⁄₁₆ in. | Estler-Regale G.m.b.H, Germany | Gift of Edgar Kaufmann, Jr., Digital image, The Museum of Modern Art, New York/Scala, Florence

Ludwig Mies van der Rohe | *Barcelona Chair*, 1929 | Stainless steel bars, leather-upholstered cushions |
29 ⅜ x 29 ¼ x 29 ¾ in. | Knoll International, New York, New York | Digital Image © The Museum of Modern Art/Licensed by
SCALA / Art Resource, New York

The early modernists saw this potential and took advantage of it. In 1927, one of the fathers of modern architecture, Ludwig Mies van der Rohe, created a cantilevered tubular steel chair,[3] which distilled the zeitgeist of the International Style into a physical object, becoming almost at once a symbol of the Bauhaus. The chair relied on the strength of its materials to balance on two legs rather than four, perfectly supporting Mies's "less is more" philosophy. Elegant yet cold, it carried a message about the future as an embodiment of trust in technology.

With the introduction of the Barcelona Chair in 1929, Mies further championed his beliefs to different ends. Made for the Barcelona International Exposition, the chair was intended to serve as seating for the king and queen of Spain, while its accompanying stool was conceived of for their attendants. This classical hierarchical arrangement paid homage to the chair's history as an object of power, from the throne to the "chairman," a reminder that until recent times, the chair was a privilege, not an entitlement.

The luxurious materials and regal form of the Barcelona Chair tap into that history while upholding modernist values. With its commanding presence and broad carriage, it is far less precarious than its cousin. Instead, it conveys stability, refinement, and order, attributes fit for a ruling class, and is as much modernist sculpture as furniture. It echoes the same philosophy as Mies's buildings. God is in the details.

A quarter century later, at a panel entitled "Problems of the Creative Artist," Charles Eames also addressed the ideological importance of the chair, urging his audience to consider every decision they made as artists as a question of morality because "we impose our creations on society." He and his wife, Ray, took these words to heart in their design work with the mantra "getting the best to the most number of people for the least."[4] Their utopian vision took the shape of molded Fiberglas and plywood chairs: mass-produced quality design that anyone could afford, espousing the ethos of a period in which postwar prosperity suggested that every family could live the American dream: a home, a college education, a car in every garage. These chairs echoed the Eameses' conviction, and so successful was the couple at marrying function with sophisticated style that the Eames Lounge Chair, less populist but revealing the Eameses' obsession with ergonomics, might be the only truly iconic easy chair in design history.

Charles Eames | *Armchair (model DAR)*, 1948–1950 | Fiberglas-reinforced polyester, steel rod, rubber shockmounts, plastic glides | 30¼ x 25 x 23¾ in. | Herman Miller, Inc., Zeeland, Michigan | Digital Image © The Museum of Modern Art/Licensed by SCALA / Art Resource, New York

Interestingly, the Eameses' colleague George Nelson felt that the many studies on ergonomics pointed to a different problem, one in which the chair was not so much the culprit as the victim of our misuse: "A really astonishing amount of effort and money has been expended by one institution or another to ascertain the average proportions of the human posterior, proper reclining positions and so on, and much of it has been embodied in the seating developed for the latest trains and planes," he observed, but "I have yet to find a seat on either which does not become excruciatingly uncomfortable after several hours. The point here is that seating is a time problem as well as a matter of carving out a shape in space."[5]

He went on to exploit this idea in his best-known design, declaring proudly that "the slat bench is a completely satisfactory seating piece for fifteen or twenty minutes ... but heaven help the person who has to spend an evening on it." Clearly more the cynic than Eames, he remarked that he had designed the bench for his waiting room to deter guests from overstaying their welcome, as if to say, "If I have not seen you by now, I don't intend to." It is worth noting that Nelson went on to create his Action Office in 1964, which among other components featured a standing desk—acknowledgment that our sitting problem was growing unwholesome even then. Regrettably, the idea never took off.

Designed by George Nelson | *Platform Bench,* Designed 1946 | Birch | 14 x 18½ x 72¼ in. | Herman Miller Furniture Co., Zeeland, Michigan | Gift of Joseph H. Makler, Jr., 1978.141, The Art Institute of Chicago

Like Nelson's Slat Bench, the electric chair alluded to by Gord Peteran in this volume similarly reminds us that the chair is not always docile, and that even anonymous chairs communicate, though their purposes may be less obvious. I recall that my grandfather, a police inspector, was once called to testify in front of a grand jury. At six foot two, he was not a small man, yet he found his feet dangling beneath him as he took the stand, and it made an impression not easily forgotten. He felt his very insignificance, and he surmised this was exactly how he was meant to feel.

At the turn of the twenty-first century, one can hardly call oneself a designer without a chair to one's name, and the aspirations of thousands, distilled into chair form, fill the great annals of design: Frank Lloyd Wright's chairs reflect his rigid construct of the world, with our ideal form measured in the straightness of its back; Eero Saarinen's soft, curving forms embrace the body; Les Lalanne's bird rockers and crocodile settees declare an impulsive exuberance and romance with the world. Every chair is as individual as its maker. Yet one must ask, how many chairs today hold up to those clear convictions of the past? To me, the words of Alessandro Mendini, from a 2015 interview, may sum up our present predicament best: "Now there is no more ideology. All the world is very confused, all the world is very violent."[6]

The chair is not always docile,

and even anonymous chairs communicate,

though their purposes may be less obvious.

Forget comfort. Our obsession with ergonomics belies the weakness of our muscles. It's no surprise that the icons of modern design are by and large not easy chairs—they were created by ideologues who knew that progress means never getting too comfortable. We live in the age of the chair, and it's time we consider what that says about us. As designer-critic Ralph Caplan points out, "A chair is the first thing you need when you don't really need anything, and is therefore a peculiarly compelling symbol of civilization. For it is civilization, not survival, that requires design."[7] So the next time you prepare to slouch down into your seat, take a moment to appreciate its joinery, its curves, the matching of the wood grain in its back, the qualities of a creation well made. And if it doesn't have any of those things, ask yourself: What does this chair say about the world we live in, and is this the world we want to live in?

Nora Atkinson
Lloyd Herman Curator of Craft
Smithsonian American Art Museum's Renwick Gallery

NOTES

1. Jennifer K. Nelson, R.D., L.D., and Katherine Zeratsky, R.D., L.D., "Do You Have 'Sitting Disease'?," Mayo Clinic, July 25, 2012; *Ergotron JustStand Survey & Index Report*, Ergotron Inc., 2013.

2. Martin Eidelberg, "Charting the Iconic Chair," in *The Eames Lounge Chair: An Icon of Modern Design* (London and New York: Merrell Publishers; Grand Rapids, Mich.: Grand Rapids Art Museum, 2006), 9.

3. Mies van der Rohe's cantilevered steel chair was based on sketches by Dutch designer Mart Stam, but refined Stam's design by taking advantage of the steel's elasticity.

4. Daniel Ostrof, "Introduction," in *An Eames Anthology: Articles, Film Scripts, Interviews, Letters, Notes, and Speeches* (New Haven, CT: Yale University Press, 2015), xvi.

5. George Nelson, "Styling, Organization-Design," *Arts & Architecture*, Aug. 1947, 24.

6. "There Is No More Ideology in Design, Says Alessandro Mendini," *Dezeen* magazine, June 26, 2015.

7. Ralph Caplan, *By Design, 2nd edition: Why There Are No Locks on the Bathroom Doors in the Hotel Louis XIV and Other Object Lessons* (New York: Fairchild, 2004).

The Elegance of Brilliant Intention

*O*n the Edge of Your Seat: Chairs for the 21st Century* throws a lot more than a spotlight on the world of relaxation. A lot more than slouching in the lounge. Intrepid enough to dissect the living environment, it's an uninhibited collision of disparate artistic invention. Look for a heady bunch of beta prototypes crammed with serious panache, from the luxurious to the shameless.

Resting our bones, easing gravity, remains ubiquitous enough. So integral to our being that we give scant thought to why the lowly seat, a means to an end, continues to inspire so much curiosity, if not devotion. The purpose of *On the Edge of Your Seat: Chairs for the 21st Century,* as I understand the exhibition, is to highlight up-to-date work of visionary excellence, identify the exceptional in character. Throughout my career I've designed chairs. I'm a maker. I've spent time at the bench and "wrestled" the chair from multiple perspectives—in the context of the industrial sector and as a woodworker immersed in the arts.

A few thoughts: A chair can carry all sorts of messages. Take Beth Krensky's ceremonial opus, *Portable Sanctuary* (displayed in this exhibit in a video), which features a chair that does just that. Strapped to the back of a "wanderer," it's hefted into the wilds during a personal quest for "resonance." Carved into the wooden frame is a sacred text. We see the chair harnessed as an agent of restful reflection, a prophetic talisman. There's much to be gleaned here.

Michelle Holzapfel, in a grand essay written for the book *Turning to Art in Wood: A Creative Journey*, a publication celebrating twenty-five years of The Center for Art in Wood (formerly the Wood Turning Center), had this to say about the object and its latent power (in our case the chair):

They make us who we are:
objects of attention, scorn or admiration.

Returning to *On the Edge of Your Seat: Chairs for the 21st Century*, I was struck, gazing at the field, by the diversity of themes, the wide artistic reach, the evident technical refinement. One excellent example is a production chair succinctly conceived by Justin Bailey, whose point of inspiration thematically alludes to early biplanes. Made to furnish a dining establishment with aeronautical decor, it's constructed from aluminum, plywood, and canvas, a reference to aircraft construction.

Another interesting conception, this one by Christy Oates, consists of a dynamic chair flattened and hung on the wall, which can later pop forth unfolded, whenever needed. Transgressing between painting and sculpture, it's also a digital progeny.

These are works that reach deep into the social fabric—as no object is more relevant than the one designed for, and of, the present. That's been voiced before but never as well as by Gregor Paulsson, the theoretician who famously hastened the charge that transfigured design in the mid-1930s: "We are looking for forms that are suitable and natural for our age, we are looking for a close link with the fine arts and with the finest gifts of nature, we want to give people the better homes they need, which will leave them with some energy to cultivate their intellectual gifts."[1]

Along these lines, a functional semiarmchair (the *Baleen Chair*) by Adrian Ferrazzutti draws elegantly from nature and unabashedly trades on traditional methods of handling the body. From a distance, it's reminiscent of a Windsor chair, reenvisioned with slats and bent wood. Seen in detail, its arched curves and novel three-point suspension project a stylish profile.

Christy Oates | *Facet Chair*, 2012 | Plywood, maple and sapele wood veneers | 16 x 16 x 33 in.

However, it is our moment in time, ironic or not. We are catalytic poster children centered within modernism's modernity, either relegated by post-modern apathy or flanked by metamodern desire. Nevertheless, our creative trajectory persists, typified by habits of appropriation, the merging of heterogeneous styles, decontextualization, and the recidivism of history. Recently, Laura Hoptman, curator of *The Forever Now: Contemporary Painting in an Atemporal World*, elaborated on the phenomena for the Museum of Modern Art in New York. She borrowed the word *atemporal* from the science fiction writer William Gibson in a formative effort to parse the scene: "Atemporal art might be summarized by saying today's art is free of singular progression, of theoretical track, or easy definition, and how agnostic it is toward social apprehension."

True of *On the Edge of Your Seat: Chairs for the 21st Century*, the show. Which is legitimized, I think, if one first acknowledges the seriousness of art making, of artists who insist that the activity and labor of the creative engagement should be embraced in the moment and understood firmly as life living. And second, that "invention" seen as art is in fact integral to life making. That the labor itself is timeless, a source of enduring power to the maker.

Applicable to those artists whose satirical use of the chair deliberately relegates it to that of a motif or symbol. Whose neoromantic innocence forestalls ridicule through informed naïveté in the search for a pragmatic idealism. Works as artifacts that brave the discourse, that frame within the social critique.

True of Lauren Kalman's work, which is notable for her bold deployment of chairs as props in a performative setting. Her brief simultaneously shields and stages the innocent body, ingeniously highlighting sui generis poses, imaged with photographs. Her motive: to reenact with contemporary emphasis Adolf Loos's "Ornament and Crime," which decries embellishment as degenerate, perennially regressive for women.

Joshua Torbick's chair, *Restructured,* is an eloquent and outstanding mythical response to an incident that resulted in physical trauma. A chair constructed but deliberately damaged by fire, functionally repaired, then put right prosthetically. A design of heartbreaking pathos, of biographical triumph over tragedy.

Jack Larimore, with a sleight of hand, confronts the idea of the chair, wrapped up in a binary sculpture. The stump of a tree clutches a column of timber salvaged from a beam. The resonant piece appropriates recycled wood, which prompted a statement. He says: "There exists a sensuous relationship between old log and old timber."

A long time ago someone carved the leg of a stool into the beak of a goose. An object enriched that gains added identity, that reveals the artistic sensibility of the maker. A joyous example of utilitarian labor made tolerable. We feel the "presence" of anthropomorphic design, which comes subtly "to life" as our attention uncodes subjectively. True of Michaela Stone's *Seated Springbok*. A primal chair of surrogate energy, one from which we might draw vehicular pleasure.

Chairs speak the language of chairs. They play the role of cultural bell-wether, intimates within their space. For us, a well-loved chair becomes an emotional placeholder, a keepsake, a personality. Your ancestor's chair, handed down, cherished, old and worn, is more than a family friend.

As with all works of art, "intention" is everything. However, with chairs, this ultimate prize, I can attest, is Promethean, a contest. So now chair bodgers all, designers, I view your work with admiration. You have my utmost respect, as well as empathy, for I know the pitfalls.

Last note: I revere elegance. Elegance of execution, a form of roused discrimination. For me the term means "paramount." With that in mind, enjoy *On the Edge of Your Seat: Chairs for the 21st Century*, the elegance of brilliant intention. Let the labor of your life—upright makers young and old—no matter how atemporal, unearth the secret entire, the light of pleasant hours.

Jasper Brinton
Principal, Brinton Design

NOTE

1.   The attributed quote from *Modern Swedish Design: Three Founding Texts* (New York: The Museum of Modern Art, 2008).

Formal Thoughts on Sitting Figures

While considering the different objects, drawings, installations, videos, and texts in this catalogue, I was reminded of an anecdote about the French surrealist poet André Breton. During his travels through Mexico in 1938, Breton commissioned a chair—sometimes recalled as a table—from a local carpenter. He gave the craftsman a sketch drawn in perspective of the chair he wanted, as a guide. When the chair was delivered to Breton from the workshop, he found a strange object: as in the drawing, the rear legs were dramatically shorter than the front, and the seat tapered at an uncomfortable angle. Where the poet had intended to convey depth and mass according to Renaissance conventions of perspective and vision, the craftsman offered instead a direct translation that identified the constraints of Breton's visual language. The same image, seen by two sets of eyes, referred to two radically different physical objects. Like Breton's carpenter, the artists and craftspeople included in this catalogue offer new thoughts on the distance between forms and ideas—between a chair as a useful object, and the histories, bodies, and places it helps to shape in the world.

History is a key ingredient for many of these artists, through the acts of homage, celebration, and revision that underscore their practices to process a lingering anxiety of historical influence. With varied approaches, they confront the past with reverence and skepticism to ask how inherited forms, styles, and narratives can shape the present.

For some, history is a playground to be mined for ideas. The eclectic history of design is an important resource for makers like Laura Mays, who adjust historic sources to suit modern tastes. Her *Ample* armchair was made to echo the protective, enclosed shape of the domed medieval English porter's chair that envelops a sitter in a warm cocoon-like space for comfort. That such a form is achieved using a distinctly modernist vocabulary of smoothed, planar wood indicates the comfort with which an emerging generation of craftspeople hopscotch through history, selecting and recombining elements into an earnest bricolage. History is an open book of inspiration for Mays and her cohort, rather than a script set in stone.

Laura Mays | *Ample*, 2015 | Ash, narra, upholstery | 46 x 28 x 32 in.

For others, like Stoel Burrowes, history exists as an active participant in the present, forcing the craftsman to consider the past when salvaging elements for a contemporary moment. As a pair, his *"A" Back Windsor* and *Metal Cat's Cradle* highlight a cautious give and take between past and present. *"A" Back Windsor* invokes the form of a historic Windsor chair with its materials, construction technique, and painted finish, yet updates the form with an eye for geometric abstraction. With straight front and rear legs that converge on the peaked crest rail, the chair has a modernist, triangular A-frame silhouette at odds with the sinuous, organic lines of its historic precedent. *Metal Cat's Cradle* adopts the same geometric organization but articulates the A-frame structure with bent tubular steel and a seat of woven elastic cords. Taken together, these chairs offer pointedly different reactions to the meeting of historic form and contemporary practice. While *"A" Back Windsor* invokes the authority of historic technique and materials, *Cat's Cradle* highlights a disconnect between period intent and contemporary realization. In the eighteenth century, when the form achieved popularity, a Windsor chair wrought by hand of oak, ash, and poplar was an inexpensive object made of humble materials for everyday use. *Cat's Cradle* echoes the spirit of the historic object in its inexpensive industrial materials to become a contemporary analogue. To make a Windsor chair for the twenty-first century, Burrowes highlights the divergent strands of form and practice that can take the same idea in different directions.

Materials have memories for craftspeople who make careful use of the histories and narratives suggested by their media. For Jordan Gehman, found objects act as a starting point for an examination of function, memory, and use. The *Booster* chair comes from his *Street Furniture* series. For this series, the artist scavenges wooden objects from the urban landscape, then repairs, adapts, and in some instances repatriates the altered objects back into the street. The *Booster* chair began as a child-size chair that Gehman adapted with the addition of a higher seat to function comfortably for a taller sitter. That the found objects from this series are altered and returned to the same context offers a distinctive critique to ideas of value and exchange of useful objects. Using straightforward techniques to transform found detritus into functional objects, Gehman resists shows of technical virtuosity and luxurious materiality normally associated with value in crafted objects. Instead, the artist carefully considers his intervention into found materials, minimally transforming them to preserve evidence of their histories in the finished piece.

The fraught relationship between chairs and sitters opens up important avenues of inquiry for a number of artists included in this volume, illustrating the potential for a carefully conceived chair to influence the mind and body of a user. With a critical hand, these artists identify the ways that traditional thinking about chairs can reinforce inherited patterns of behavior, and offer new ways to consider the needs of diverse bodies.

The science of ergonomics looms large over many of the chairs illustrated in this volume, with different makers offering different ways to mediate the health of a sitter's body through the form of a constructed chair. Takahiro Yoshino offers a unique approach to this consideration with his maple *Zen Round Back Chair* to encourage the practice of meditative zazen sitting. According to the artist, each chair of this model is fit to the pelvis and spine of the sitter to guide a specific posture in which the "head and pelvis are in perfect alignment, reducing the stress you encounter throughout the day." The bespoke refinement of Yoshino's work navigates a delicate balance between the specificity of his form and the ubiquity of his design references. The *Zen Round Back Chair* suggests the common stacking office chair, yet each one is crafted by hand with the precise body of the intended sitter in mind. His emphasis on zazen practices also highlights the cultural specificity of ergonomic considerations in chair design. While the language of ergonomics is often medical and anatomical, Yoshino offers a way in which the physical comfort of the seated body intersects with spiritual practice behaviors of a sitter.

In her union of craft, sculpture, performance, and photography, Lauren Kalman explores the ways a sitter can react against codes of gender, value, and propriety embedded in the forms of beloved designs. Drawn from the *Composition with Ornament and Object* photographs from her *But if the Crime Is Beautiful* series, *Composition 18* confronts the meeting of modernist design— dogmatically devoid of ornament, per Adolf Loos's 1908 lecture from which the series derives its name—and the gilded, nude, female body. As Kalman argues, the same mid-century modern objects invoked as status objects by collectors and decorators regulate and proscribe female sexuality. The uncomfortable union of gilded bodies, turned and contorted into floating abstract ornaments, and rigid machine-made lines of modernist design is used to display the tension between the sculptural form of a useful object and the bodies that interact with it. The molded plywood chair she photographs was created to allow certain kinds of use. An adult body of average size can sit in it with ease, upright with a straight back. By illustrating the disconnect between ornamented, eroticized female bodies and unornamented forms designed to accommodate certain bodies in limited postures, Kalman identifies the subtle politics of chairs that discourage specific patterns of behavior along gendered lines.

The chairs made by Joshua Torbick offer a related meditation on the ways that traditional chair forms presume specific sitters and exclude others. His *Wedged In* grew from the maker's experience of losing a leg after a motorcycle accident. He began crafting furniture to address the specific physical needs of his body with an eye toward the role furniture plays in structuring social interaction. The *Wedged In* chair functions by supporting the body upright in a standing position without relying on lower body strength to regulate posture. *Wedged In*—which developed its formal vocabulary from the maker's examination of prosthetic limbs and the materials of "executive furniture"—supports the user at standing height for "meaningful work and social engagement." Falling somewhere between chair, stool, and prosthetic, Torbick's project serves as a pointed rejoinder to designers and makers who create furniture for sociability without accounting for the diversity of bodies that will use them. Finding traditional forms lacking, he considered his own physical abilities when inventing new seating forms to allow diverse users access to social engagement.

Meditations on place and space root many of the artists and craftspeople making chairs. While it might be taken as a given that chairs and other useful objects shape the character and potential of their environments, a number of these projects examine the inner working and meanings of that effect.

The chair becomes a landscape for Sheri Crider and Nina Dubois, collaborating under the assumed name T. Fitzallan. Their monumental installation *Drift #1* places sitters in a fabricated landscape of undulating walls, flat plateaus for seating, and the honeycombed edges of accreted industrial materials. Recalling the Dutch architect Rem Koolhaas's notion of *junkspace*—"what remains after modernization has run its course"[1]—the pair looks to transform the ubiquitous and inexpensive materials of the contemporary built environment. They do so to identify the environmental impact of inexpensive construction materials quickly assembled into structures and just as quickly sent to the landfill. In its formal language, *Drift #1* balances the romantic notions of the western American landscape against a thoughtful material-driven examination of accelerated handmade alteration to the same landscape. Instead of creating a chair as a discrete form, Crider and Dubois create an environmental installation to envelop the seat and sitter. To drive home the notion that a shift in the built environment from longevity to disposable impermanence is reshaping the natural landscape, Crider and Dubois created a seat within a simulated landscape made of cast-off materials.

Beth Krensky offers a related meditation in the video of her performance of *Portable Sanctuary #1*, taking the chair out of a domestic or gallery context and into the western landscape as part of the artist's practice of wandering. For this piece, Krensky attached leather straps to a found classroom chair and carried it on her back out of the studio and into a natural environment. Describing the parameters of her performance, the artist writes, "As I'm walking, whenever I'm ready, I put it down and sit on it, and when I see fit, I take it up again." With open-ended guidelines and a light footprint, Krensky offers a model for artist-driven environmental activism in the realm of lived practice. The found chair is adapted for portability, and when carried into a natural landscape, allows the sitter to create a temporary contemplative space without built intervention. In this way Krensky amplifies the generative relationship between sitter and chair, identifying a set of practices that give significance to the simple act of sitting; the sanctuary is not a building, or even a chair, but a movable place willed into existence by the artist. With the text of Psalm 23 engraved on the chair, the performance recalls precedents from religious history like the ascetic stylite monks who lived in contemplative isolation atop pillars in

Beth Krensky |
Portable Sanctuary #1,
2011 | Wood, leather |
37 x 17 x 27 in. |
Josh Blumental

the wilderness. Updated for contemporary conditions and concerns, Krensky highlights the way that meditative practice can transform humble objects and anonymous spaces into meaningful places.

In contrast, Misha Volf takes placelessness as the subject of his *4 x 4 Bench*. Like Crider and Dubois, Volf makes adaptive use of the vernacular materials of a globalized economy. His bench is constructed with a frame of unadorned four-by-four cedar planks strung with ratchet straps to support padded cushions, and rubber caster feet for portability. The sensibility is one of making do from the refuse of a loading dock that could be in Shanghai, Lagos, New York, or any other city where shipping containers move immense mountains of goods around the planet. Volf does so to explore the bench as a "conflicted object," wedged between the rootedness of sitting and the acceleration of global communication, trade, and migration, which allows people and goods to crisscross continents. These concerns are practical as well as theoretical, and Volf takes a nimble touch with solid form to create a useful and adaptable piece of furniture for changing contexts. It moves around a room on its casters and easily disassembles when it comes time to move from one apartment to another, or from one continent to another. Coming at a time when local practices, traditions, products, and materials are proudly touted in advertising by both individual

Misha Volf | *4 x 4 Bench*, 2015 | Eastern red cedar, ratchet straps | 32 x 60 x 31 in.

craftspeople and international retailers, Volf offers a strikingly direct confrontation of a material landscape that shows few considerations for regional context. Instead of looking to the past to define a sense of place, his *4 x 4 Bench* reacts to the globalization of materials and ideas, erasing historical distinctions between places and populations.

The makers discussed in this volume present many different ways of considering how, why, and where we sit. They revel in an eclectic array of forms and narratives freely mixed together from the past, or examine an ongoing conversation between past and present. Some explore the ways that bodies can transform the meanings embedded in chairs, while others highlight the ways that chairs can meet the needs of diverse bodies. They demonstrate the different ways that a chair can anchor and transform a place while also exploring the ways that objects can adapt to a globalized culture, eroding local distinctions. That a shared point of inspiration—a simple chair—can lead to so many different results highlights the significant role that artists and craftspeople play in decoding the meanings of the material world around us. Like André Breton's carpenter described in the beginning of this essay, they force us to consider the distance between forms and concepts and give voices to the often unspoken ideas built into the useful and beautiful around us.

Benjamin Colman
Associate Curator of American Art
at the Detroit Institute of Arts

NOTE

1.   Rem Koolhaas, "Junkspace," *October* 100 (Spring 2002), 175.

Some Observations on Twenty-First-Century Seating

From the encrusted gilt of King Tut's throne to the gleaming steel bends of Marcel Breuer's *Wassily Chair*, seating reveals a culture's preoccupations. Today, fifteen years into the twenty-first century, is no different. The more than forty objects that fill these pages illuminate a diverse culture coming to terms with past and future, stretching to accommodate new technologies and adapting, in every instance, to the changing needs of a society in flux.

Like furniture makers across time, several participants find inspiration in historically resonant works. Stoel Burrowes and Adrian Ferrazzutti, for instance, have each reimagined the Windsor chair, that multispoked amalgam of techniques and woods adopted by North American colonists from the British and seemingly reinvented in every age since. Through their hands and eyes, the Windsor chair becomes the basis for poetic reconsiderations of form and material, as in Burrowes's *"A" Back Windsor* and *Metal Cat's Cradle* chairs, or as the jumping-off point for playful imagination, as in Ferrazzutti's *Baleen Chair*, which, as the name suggests, imitates the comb-like mouth of a whale by doubling and inverting the chair's spokes and crest rail.

Adrian Ferrazzutti | *Baleen Chair*, 2013 | Wenge, satin wood | 29 x 28 x 26 in.

Unlikely as it may seem, Mira Nakashima's sculptural *Concordia Chair* is also an examination of the Windsor, though filtered through her father's own mid-century interpretation. Redacting entirely the spindles that characterize a Windsor or midcentury George Nakashima chair, her piece instead combines elements drawn from across her father's oeuvre with feedback from the members of the Concordia Chamber Players for whom the chair was designed. Squat, round, and charmingly anthropomorphic, the result is a chair that pays homage to the designs of her father, his Danish contemporaries, and, by extension, to the broader lineage of furniture history.

These thoughtful and thoughtfully divergent reinvestigations, along with contributions by Laura Mays and Fabiano Sarra, among others, call attention to the enduring value of well-made furniture of good design. By contrast, Jennifer Anderson's *Cadwalader Chair* critiques that very notion. Named for the Revolutionary War general who commissioned and owned them, Cadwalader Chairs are among the most expensive of all time, fetching well over one million dollars at auction. Remade in mud, Anderson's piece serves as a *memento mori* signaling, through its parched, cracking surface, the transience of the originals and questioning the value system that holds these antiquated objects in such high esteem.

Yet, almost equal to the impact of the old in this collection is the presence of the new. More than in any other furniture exhibition in recent memory (outside of ones devoted specifically to the topic), the artists, makers, and designers included here demonstrate a sustained embrace of digital technologies. Some pieces, like Christy Oates's beguiling laser-cut *Facet Chair*, which pops out of an ornamental wall hanging and folds into shape, are forthright elaborations of technology as didactic as they are charming. Others, such as Justin Bailey's flat-packing *Airliner Chair*, invoke digital tooling as much for its symbolic power as for its structural efficiency. Designed for an Iowa City restaurant with a biplane theme, this chair pairs contemporary technologies such as computer numerical

Mira Nakashima | *Concordia Chair*, 2003 | American black walnut | 31½ x 19½ x 16 in.

control (CNC) laser and plasma cutting with a material palette that harks to the earliest planes, creating a crisp, functional seat that harnesses the dynamic innovation of the birth of aviation without the smallest whiff of nostalgia.

Even pieces that do not incorporate digital technologies, such as Sophie Glenn's *Collapsible Stools* and Andrew Jay Rumpler's *Tatum's Lounge,* demonstrate the impact of the digital. For Glenn, the influence is direct: her handmade, flat-packing, solid wood stools are an attractive response to the notion that affordable, flat-pack design can only originate in the digital. In Rumpler's piece, the influence is more atmospheric. His homage to the legendary jazz pianist Art Tatum, grown "in the organic manner of a Tatum solo: with both order and abandon,"[1] manages to perfectly embody both the quirky appeal of Tatum's playing and the vibrant, jangly lines of low-end computer drawing programs such as Microsoft Paint.

Perhaps the clearest expression of the potential of the digital age is found in Tad Gloeckler's *Segment Rotation Seat.* Made completely with the use of CNC technology, with the same visible toolmarks that characterize Oates, Bailey, and nearly every other digital entrant, *Segment Rotation* consists of a series of stacked plywood sections attached to a rotating core like thighs to the hip. Segments can be added or subtracted as needed and have a range of motion that allows them to lock in different positions to create armrests, headrests, or backrests, as the user desires. Modular, customizable, and ergonomic, *Segment Rotation* is both a pure expression of the tool and a humanizing use of the machine.

At the heart of the adaptability provided by pieces like *Segment Rotation Seat* is an acknowledgment of the intimate relationship between furniture and the body. This notion, and the accompanying idea of furniture as a familiar, influential actor in the unfolding tableau of life—one that can translate physical experience from person to person through the angle of a backrest and the shape of a seat—is the motivation behind several of the most emotionally powerful works in this exhibition.

Take, for example, Joshua Torbick's cathartic *Restructured Chair.* Comprising a burned ash side chair mended with mismatched white appendages, the piece speaks directly to Torbick's own experience of losing a limb and his subsequent physical and psychological recovery. Scorched and listing to one side, propped on its white crutches, the chair seems awkward, wrong, "crippled." And yet, for

Joshua M. Torbick | *Restructured Chair,* 2015 | Ash | 24 x 19 x 43 in.

Torbick, its function has never been better. Its current orientation creates a perch that is easier to rise from and more comfortable for his prosthetic, a reminder that, in furniture as in clothing, one size fits all rarely does.

Rehabilitating trauma through reenactment is also the thread of Alicia Dietz's *Reintegration*, which lays bare the complexities of returning to civilian life after military service. An upholstered club chair constructed out of discarded shipping pallets, *Reintegration* at first appears familiar and unremarkable. Sitting, however, reveals a different picture.

Rising from the cushions, enveloping the sitter, is a soundscape that eerily, evocatively overlays the cheerful sounds of everyday life—the chirp of birds, the tinkling of dishes, the hum of a lawn mower—with the pulsing beat of an airplane motor, the pop of machine gun fire, and the low-bellied rumble of explosions near and far. The effect is immediate and profound; communicating through the senses, *Reintegration* does more to illuminate the seizing disorientation of post-traumatic stress than any news story ever could.

These works and the exquisite, compelling seats that join them are just a small glimpse of the vibrant field of small-scale design and studio furniture production today. They stand as a testament to the ingenuity of the makers and their ability to conjure meaning from material and technique. If they are any indication, the twenty-first century will be a good one for chairs.

Susie Silbert

Curator, historian

NOTE

1.   Andrew Jay Rumpler, Artist's Statement, *On the Edge of Your Seat* exhibit (Philadelphia, 2016)..

Plates

Jennifer Anderson

CADWALADER CHAIR

My art is rooted in tradition yet fueled by experimentation. I find technology to be both seductive and repulsive. I create functional objects that people live and interact with on a daily basis. These objects not only serve the basic needs of people but are also the primary vehicles for my self-expression.

My most recent work focuses on translating iconic pieces of furniture into mud. By taking a material that is otherwise thought of as worthless and translating it into highly regarded objects, I am asking people to reconsider their relationships with domestic objects.

At the root of this work lies my struggle to feel grounded and connected to the ever-changing and fast-paced world in which we live. The materials I work with are natural and therapeutic. My process is slow, methodical, and often tedious. It is precisely this pace that makes me feel reconnected to the earth. The completed objects stimulate your sense of sight, smell, and touch.

Concentrating on a genre with a long history of tradition creates an extra challenge because it is stereotyped into a specific category. It is specifically these stereotypes that fuel my desire to further the discipline of my field and to break down the stereotypes that categorize the work I make.

Cadwalader Chair,
2016 | Mud, steel |
37 x 22 x 26 in. |
Heather McCalla

Justin
Bailey

AIRLINER CHAIR

Originally created for a reimagining of the interior of the Airliner, an Iowa City establishment that is currently a sports bar. I wanted to envision the space as living up to the imagery and aesthetic of its namesake, an early biplane and the associated structure. A restaurant's chairs are an opportunity to bring the aesthetic of an overall spatial design to a functional, human scale. The *Airliner Chair* was custom designed for the space, keeping with the lightweight, linear, and open feel.

The shape of biplanes provided some guidance in the placement of line framework. My interpretation of the body of the airplane is a widening progression that created an outer structure from lines. I used that for legs of the chair, moving lines to account for the human body as needed. I also wanted to bring in visual movement to the frame, helping to lead the eye through the framework in addition to highlighting all the necessary lines.

As the design of the chair progressed, it became easier to imagine building as a physical prototype. The materials it was to be made in were drawn directly from early aircraft: metal, wood, and canvas. The canvas would provide the seat and back surface, referencing back to how it was stretched over a wooden framework in early gliders to form the surface area of wings. Metal and wood would be the linear structure supporting the canvas. Steel was placed on the outside profiles with two layers of one-quarter-inch plywood encased inside another steel piece. Computer numerical control (CNC) technology was incorporated to make production easier—used to plasma cut eighteen-gauge

Airliner Chair, 2015 |
Powder-coated steel,
plywood, canvas |
32 x 22 x 23 in.

mild steel sheets and to laser cut plywood in the side profiles and linking bars. The individual pieces are assembled together using riveting screw posts placed at linear intersections and short intervals, also referencing the use of rivets in airplane construction dating back to the Second World War.

The final version of the *Airliner Chair* is able to pack flat. The five front-facing crossbars can be removed with a flat-head screwdriver, allowing the side profile pieces to collapse with the canvas held between. The crossbars use an icon-driven numbering system to indicate their placement on the chair when assembling, as well. A system of dashes at their centers relays the number of the bar, relating to its height and position on the chair. Additionally, in the final version of the chair, the sheet metal has been powder coated white, preserving it as a material and also highlighting the use of line as it has been matched with the darkened, burned edges of the laser-cut plywood. The powder coating also allows for variations on the color of the frame in production, which could be a great way to involve the chair in more dynamic spatial compositions.

Bob
Brox

ENTRENCHING [S]TOOL

While the twenty-first century thus far has been an interesting one with its wars and panic intertwined with smartphones and yoga, no one can guess how it will end, but, as it is, most of the world still squeaks by on a few dollars a day and doesn't sit on walnut or leather. A good bit of the "needs and nature" of twenty-first-century seating certainly arises from what those masses sit on.

My work takes me to some of the poorest places on earth, and when I am offered a seat, it is usually a stackable plastic chair or a simple plank bench— furniture pumped out of a distant factory or swatted together by a bunch of boys working under a thatched canopy—and it is furniture that works well. But once in a while something special might come out, a real gem, like a chair made from an old wooden cart wheel or a lounger cut from a rusty oil drum. Never duplicated—the poor man's one-off. Cobbled together from the precious heap of things with no pending use but considered much too valuable to throw away. Stylish tags like "green," "repurposed," or "recycled" never enter the maker's mind. Their thoughts are much more pure and their craft drips of their way of life. Although I am very far from being that kind of poor, I hope I learned something while watching from my perch.

The use of shovel handles and scrapped tire to construct the *Entrenching [S]tool* may be symbolic of resource-efficient societies where manual labor is how things get done and where little is wasted, but they were also chosen because they are simply fine materials for this task. The sturdy shovel handles coincidentally work well for legs and their ergonomic curves add a measure of

Entrenching [S]tool, 2015 | Shovel handles, used tire rubber, cotter pins, washers, screws, oil finish | 19 x 17 x 15 in.

grace. The seat, stitched from rubber peeled from an old tire that could also have been used to make sandals or a water pump gasket, is soft yet durable, and this piece in particular has an appealing hieroglyphic-like pattern to it. The most common of fasteners hold it all together.

I have never been asked to sit on something quite like the *Entrenching [S]tool* but I think I could have. My aim was to capture a spirit, but perhaps the best I could do was mimic it, as the stool is a product of my circumstances. The rubber I found in a far-off village in Myanmar, but the handles I bought at a garden center because it was easy and I wanted them to be all the same. My sensibilities (and probably yours) insisted that those handles be sanded smooth and oiled. However, I am content with this work being a celebration of that spirit. I also think it is a good piece of furniture.

If someone were to "experience" my chair, I hope it would be an experience of comfort and security. I think it gives that. Perhaps they would ponder its simplicity. For them to consider what it is made of might be nice (... shovels ... tires ... that's neat). Beyond this, though maybe unlikely, I would hope it would help them think about the world, as it is.

Stoel
Burrowes

"A" BACK WINDSOR

The *"A" Back Windsor* is a well-crafted design from the classic Windsor seating tradition. Because the legs pass through or by the seat, the tension and compression of parts is changed without loss of function. A classic poem form deconstructed in free verse.

Careful choices of wood, joinery, and human factors inspired this chair. White oak legs with strong, straight grain pass through the seat and support the seat on a wider leg profile under the seat. The poplar seat is more easily carved and the ash crest rail is steam bent. The wood and joinery choices are traditional Windsor technology. The traditional black-on-red milk paint finish provides another rhyme with history.

This dining or side chair has an upright, nearly puritanical feel. I wish the sitter and the observer to be intrigued and pleased by both the comfort and the juxtaposition of parts.

METAL CAT'S CRADLE

The *Metal Cat's Cradle* is shown as a sketch model at 3":1' scale. Based on some of the same technical considerations as the previous *"A" Back Windsor*, the wooden *Cat's Cradle* was exhibited in the Home Exhibit in the 2015 Furniture Society Symposium. The photographic details show the wooden *Cat's Cradle*. I propose to make a metal frame of 1" tubing with colorful bungee woven across the seat and back. The comfort provided by the elastic bungee and the relaxed form and angles makes this a special seating experience. Especially, the balance of bright color and dark metal functions to make surprise.

"A" Back Windsor, 2012 |
White oak, ash, poplar,
oil and wax finish |
38 x 27 x 20 in.

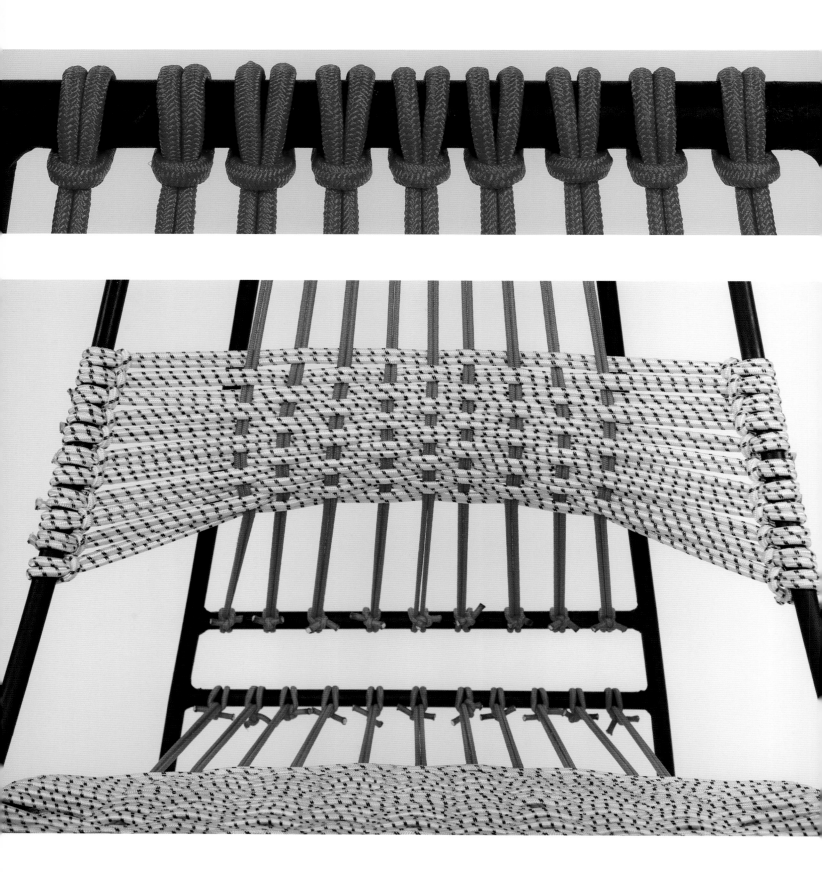

Metal Cat's Cradle, 2014 | Metal, bungee seat and back | 39 x 26 x 28 in.

Sheri Crider & Nina Dubois

DRIFT #1

Drift #1 is the first of a series of sculptural installations that transform materials destined for a local landfill to large-scale sculpture. The artists share a deep dedication to sculptural production that is embedded in a discourse of climate change through a historical lens of materials and land use. Both artists' grandfathers were notable in their resourcefulness and respect for resources. The artists' use of the moniker *T. Fitzallan*—based on a hybrid of the artists' grandfathers' names—is to emphasize significant changes in the availability and the subsequent devaluation of materials in the last fifty years. Both artists look to physical space for a deeper understanding of human interaction with materials, space, and light.

Drift #1, 2015 |
Hollow-core doors,
wood glue | 10 x 12 x 16 ft.

Alicia Dietz

REINTEGRATION

Serving in the US Army for over ten years as an officer, Blackhawk helicopter pilot, maintenance test pilot, and company commander, I led soldiers in the minus-sixty-degree-Fahrenheit temperatures of Alaska and in the 130-degree-Fahrenheit-plus deserts of Egypt. I flew missions over the huts of Baghdad, the moose of Alaska, and the Egyptian/Israeli border in the Sinai. I served with men and women from all walks of life.

The transition from my military career to civilian life continues even today, four years after my last day in uniform. Many days, I hear a sound in my domestic landscape that takes me immediately back to my military days. It is the constant soundtrack that plays in my head.

Wanting the viewer to get just a glimpse of how a soldier's memory fades in and out of reality, I made this chair an invitation. My goal is for the viewer to walk away and perhaps start a conversation with a friend, a relative, or even a stranger about his or her reintegration into civilian life.

Audio is an important component to this piece. Coming from a parabolic speaker, the sounds are heard only when sitting in the chair. Life continues to go on around the participant—a group walks by; two gentlemen have a conversation; a baby cries. All compete with the audio, fighting for the viewer's attention.

The chair sits on a wood-floor installation. Walking across this floor, you want and expect it to feel familiar. But this piece looks and feels different, giving a sense of being in the home but also somewhere far away. In what is

Reintegration, 2015 | Oak pallets, audio, fabric, LED lighting | chair 26 x 26 x 28 in.; flooring 6 x 10 x 16 ft. | Jeremy Zietz

an unstable transition for many veterans, I found myself trying to find a place in the world and to grasp a sense of purpose—in need of a map. I created cut-outs of various cities that I routinely flew over as a pilot. These are how I remember seeing the cities at night—specks of light with vast areas of openness surrounding them. The floor cracks and creaks as you walk over it, moves beneath you, and gives you the sense that you are high above while simultaneously standing right on top.

Walking across the floor to sit in the chair, the viewer becomes immersed in another world. Domestic sounds of a thunderstorm and cleaning dishes transition into mortar explosions and the sound of a rifle being taken apart. The sounds illustrate how seemingly meaningless moments can trigger a past event. There is a dichotomy of feeling physically comfortable in the chair while concurrently feeling uneasy about the noises that are heard.

The chair is made from old wooden pallets. A pallet in the process of becoming a chair; a soldier in the process of becoming a civilian. Pallets are made of wood that individually cannot support a heavy load. However, when constructed in a particular way, those thin slabs of wood can hold an object much heavier than itself. They are analogous to a soldier.

This chair is the beginning of a journey to expose the visible and invisible wounds. To explore my own thoughts about what war does to soldiers' bodies, to their minds, to their souls, and to their humanity.

Jack R. Elliott

TRIAKONTA25 — WBC

The Triakonta structural system of nodes and struts was developed at Cornell University as an investigation into a low embodied energy architectural system for building. It is named after the rhombic triacontahedron that it uses for nodes. Rather than use spheres that are custom drilled for each application, a uniform polyhedron with flat faces was sought. This would limit the spatial arrangements but would create a systematized set of struts.

Examples of polyhedral nodes from industry usually include Archimedean solids such as truncated cubes or truncated octahedrons. However, these have very limited internal angular relationships, resulting in a limited set of forms.

Instead, a thirty-sided convex polyhedron known as a rhombic triacontahedron was selected, hence the product name "Triakonta." In the case of this chair, "25" refers to the metric measurement across the opposite flats of the node, and the initials "WBC" are for "wing-back chair." This shape can produce standard orthogonal structures with right angular relationships, but more significantly, it can also create triangular, pentagonal, and hexagonal arrangements.

In addition to this geometric complexity, the Triakonta system is unique among geodesic structural systems for its use of wood for the struts of this geodesic system. Typical geodesic systems rely

Triakonta25—WBC, 2010 | Cast aluminum, stainless steel, black locust | 32 x 18 x 24 in.

on metal tubing, precise and uniform but with little character. The Triakonta system exploits the linear grain configuration and familiar look of the natural material while allowing for its irregularities of surface within a standardized set of building components. The structures have a "natural" look but have very tight tolerances.

In order to test the system, a quarter-scale test-of-concept set of parts was produced. The wood components are made from locally sourced black locust, a wood known for its high strength, low value, and good machinability. The end anchors are made from stainless steel bolts captured in an aluminum sleeve in such a way that the bolt is free to rotate and move along its axis. The sleeve is inserted into a hole drilled into the end of the strut and a perpendicular dowel pin is pressed into a hole drilled in the side of the strut to fix the sleeve into the wood. A stainless steel nut is welded to the bolt over which a hexagonally broached stainless steel coupling nut is fitted. The bolt is turned into a node by rotating the coupling nut.

Geometrically, connecting rhombic triacontahedrons generates golden relationships between the component lengths. For example, connecting three rhombic triacontahedrons with straight line segments normal to their faces produces triangles that are either equilateral or isosceles. The isosceles are of two types: narrow or wide. In either case, the lengths of the sides of the isosceles triangles are related to their bases by the golden ratio or its inverse. Thus, the rhombic triacontahedron produces a three-dimensional system using only three different lengths: short, medium, and long, each greater than the preceding one by a factor of 1.618. The result is great configurational variety with few standardized components. Additionally, the system is designed for disassembly, so that the structure can be modified to accommodate changing conditions or, at the end of life, can be completely dismantled and reconfigured for a new site or set of conditions. In the case of the chair, it could be reconfigured into a table.

When configured into the *Triakonta25—WBC,* a chair of pure structure is created. In fact, the chair is structure. As an open structure, the chair is also air, allowing light to pass through it. The *Triakonta25—WBC* challenges the user's idea of "chairness." It is a modern seating device of unique geometries, but the wood gives it a sense of warmth and familiarity.

Dugan Essick

GEISHA BAR STOOL

The inspiration for the *Geisha Bar Stool* came to me some forty years ago when I first sketched it on a shipping card. My goal was a chair with simple minimal design and flowing lines. I was happy with the design but wasn't sure how to make it strong enough to be a functional chair. The card was cast aside in the back of my tool box and forgotten. Then several years ago, after a move, I was setting up my new shop and found the card. The design still appealed to me and I once again began thinking about building it.

Over the years I had the good fortune to be involved with many boatbuilding projects and had gained both an understanding and respect for the structural properties of composites. I have found that by combining these modern materials I can do things not previously possible using traditional woodworking methods. My first attempt to build this chair using composites was combining a rigid layup of carbon fiber and Baltic birch plywood. It is very easy to regulate the stiffness of the chair by using more or less carbon fiber in the layup. This allows me to build a very stiff chair or a chair with a little spring in it.

In this chair the wood I chose was a marine-grade mahogany. The darker color adds richness and creates interesting patterns with the laminations. I also chose a moderately heavy layup of carbon fiber to give the chair a good stiff feel. The seat is sculptured for comfort but also blends well with the curves of the chair. I find the curve of the lumbar support slats to be a very attractive curve and choose to accentuate it by carrying the line down past the seat of the chair.

Geisha Bar Stool, 2015 |
**Marine mahogany,
carbon fiber |
44 x 21 x 24 in.**

I've tried to keep the lines simple and graceful with soft faceted organic transitions between connecting pieces, and it is my hope that others will also be drawn to the gentle flowing simplicity of the chair and the interesting patterns emphasized by the use of plywood. I'm also pleased to create a little curiosity and wonder at looking at something that looks like it won't work but is actually very strong. After finishing my first version of this chair and showing it to my customer, she immediately replied, "It looks like a geisha on her knees." From then on it became a chair with a name.

Adrian
Ferrazzutti

SIGNATURE ARM CHAIR
FALLINGBROOK CHAIR
BALEEN CHAIR

Seeking to create something new, something challenging to make, something amazing to look at, and have it be comfortable, I have always been inspired by the chair as an object.I really get inspired from making mock-ups; I love the design process and the challenge of creating something made of lines that all work together in three dimensions simply to support a person. Beyond this function I think one spends more time looking at the chair than sitting in it, so to me a pleasing, resolved design is paramount. I work in a minimal, modern style.

Early and mid-century modern chair designs have given and continue to give me inspiration. Many of the iconic chairs were mostly designed for production and used many new materials and factory processes. Wood is my medium and old woodworking techniques and processes appeal to me, as does one-off custom work. I try to use wood in an honest way by not asking it to do what steel or plastics can. It doesn't mean I'm not trying to push the bounds of what wood can do, I just try to stop before it looks weird or wrong.

Signature Arm Chair, 2012 | Hickory, leather | 35 x 25 x 29 in.

The woods I choose for my chairs are based first on strength and flex characteristics. Second comes color.

Hickory and ash are top contenders for strength and wenge is too, but with wenge comes that fabulous black and brown color that for me really emphasizes the lines of a chair. I also love contrast, and by choosing woods like satin wood (a yellow wood) or colored leathers and a wenge frame, the combination of colors and materials can be very striking. Striking is what I'm after. I would like people to be pulled in by my chairs, their design and materials, pulled in close to discover the workmanship, fine details, and of course comfort. I would like people to then step back and look again and perhaps say "wow!"

Fallingbrook Chair, 2012 | Ash, wenge | 32 x 18 x 22 in.

Baleen Chair, 2013 |
Wenge, satin wood |
29 x 28 x 26 in.

Amy
Forsyth

TREEHOUSE CHAIR

One of my favorite things to do is to rummage through images in search of something wonderful and surprising, which I then draw in my sketchbook for future reference. This chair design began with the Bodley Bestiary, a medieval book of illuminated creatures. I drew the manticore, mostly because I liked the composition and the trees and the casual way in which a human leg was dangling from the critter's mouth.

I make my own sketchbooks, and this drawing happened to land on a page that already had an image of a distressed woman wearing a circa 1890s dress, so to incorporate the drawing of the manticore with the woman, I gave her a chair made of the trees in the background behind the manticore. I liked this chair so much that I later did a few sketches of it, trying to determine the structure of the seat.

This past fall, I took a class in "deconstructed screen printing" on fabric, and realized that I could make any pattern on upholstery that I wanted to make, and this chair came farther into focus. It's really a carving project, which I've been enjoying quite a lot lately, so I see it being carved out of basswood and painted with milk paint. The design of the tree and the various fronds will develop as I carve them. Although the original mood of the woman in the image was distressed, I see this as a comforting, protective, playful chair, oversize and silly, almost throne-like, a cross between Chairy of Pee-wee's Playhouse, John Makepeace's wonderful carved leafy chair, and a whimsical carved wooden garden.

Treehouse Chair, 2015–2016 | Basswood, paint, fabric | 68 x 35 x 25 in. | Christa Neu

Jordan
D. Gehman

BOOSTER

This series of chairs explores the value placed on the objects we keep closest.
I collect discarded wooden objects from the streets and out of dumpsters,
gathering broken chairs, ladders, headboards, scrap wood, and random materials that seem useful. These leftover materials from my neighborhood provide
me with a steady flow of new forms, content, and technical challenges. I fix
some of these objects then put them back on the street to be rediscovered by
someone else. Some are dismantled into parts that are placed in my collection
of remnants for later use, and a few are addressed carefully, repaired to the best
of my abilities.

Booster, 2012 |
Found chair,
mahogany, paint |
25 x 13 x 13 in.

Sophie Glenn

COLLAPSIBLE STOOLS

These collapsible stools were made in response to the growing trend of
flat-pack furniture typically produced through CNC (Computer Numeric
Controlled) technology, and the tradition of making solid wood furniture by
hand. Although CNC technology and its heavy use of plywood has made
producing furniture exponentially more efficient in more ways than one, there
is still a great appreciation for the one-of-a-kind aspect of furniture that was
made by hand, even if someone may not necessarily have the means of own-
ing such pieces, either because of lack of space, budget, or other factors. In
this respect, what I would like to see most when someone experiences one of
these stools is that he/she feels they can own a handmade piece of furniture
that can still be accommodating to his/her daily lifestyle, no matter what that
lifestyle may be.

I wanted the design of these stools to be relatively simple, not only for the
means of production but also for consumer use. The fabricated steel components of these stools were inspired by lift-off door hinges and are connected to
the legs using bridle joints and steel pins. All of the legs rotate on a central post,
so one could position the legs however they please and lock them into place
using thumb screws. And when not in use, the legs nestle together and pack
flat for easy storage. The seat can also be easily removed and stored away when
not in use.

The inclusion of solid wood (and particularly different kinds of solid wood)
in these stools was crucial for a number of reasons, but it was most important

Collapsible Stools, 2015 |
Various woods and
powder-coated steel |
18–22 x 12–14 in. dia.

in the design process. First, in response to CNC technology and the use of plywood, I felt it was important to make flat-pack furniture out of solid wood, to introduce a hand-built element to the stools. And with that in mind, I also wanted to introduce some traditional wood joinery in the design of these stools, which is evident in the bridle joints used to connect the legs to the steel hinges.

Overall, I think the design choices pertaining to the mechanism and overall functionality of the stools were key in creating a more "user-friendly" and less precious object, while at the same time I feel the aesthetic choices, particularly with the materials and the type of joinery used, helped make the stools feel more like a handmade and perhaps a more traditional woodworking object, and less like a computer-generated thing.

SCHOOL DESK

This piece was directly inspired by my own personal needs when living in a small space. I currently live in a two-hundred-square-foot converted garage in San Diego (which is probably the largest space that a student budget would allow), and it has been difficult at times to focus on my schoolwork in certain areas of my home, mainly because I have to use the few pieces of furniture that I own for various different functions. For example, one of two chairs that I own functions not only as a chair but also as a desk, a dining room table, and some-times a laundry basket, among other things. One can imagine that it would become difficult to finish writing an essay for one of my classes when I am also thinking about whether I have enough quarters to do my laundry.

Certainly there are others who live in similar situations, so with that in mind, I wanted to design and make a piece of furniture that was only to be used for one specific function, but was also small enough to not take up a lot of space in one's tiny apartment, house, etc. The general function and compactness of the school desk seemed to be an appropriate solution. Although the school desk is not a piece of furniture that is typically associated with the home because it is almost always seen with twenty to thirty exact replicas in a classroom setting, it is an object that many people easily recognize because of its very specific function.

Taking the school desk and re-creating it to be more appropriate in the home provided an interesting challenge in terms of design. The more formal

School Desk, 2015 | Walnut and painted steel | 30 x 24 x 35 in.

elements of the school desk are still intact, especially that of the seat and desk being attached as one unit, and that of only having access to the seat from one side, which gives directionality and forces the user to use the desk in a particular way. In terms of my choice of material, I wanted to remain true to the traditional school desk being made primarily out of wood and steel, but instead I used solid walnut as opposed to the usual plywood and fabricated a more angular steel structure instead of bending steel tube. The treatment of the steel is also quite different here from the treatment in the more traditional school desk. Instead of leaving the weld seams exposed and giving the steel a polished or chrome-plated finish, I decided to fabricate the structure as cleanly as possible and paint the steel orange. All of these decisions were made to give the school desk a much more personalized and less mass-produced appearance.

When someone sits at this desk, I would like for him/her to feel almost as if they are in an environment that is promoted by its specific functionality, rather than simply a piece of furniture that can be used for any purpose necessary.

Tad Gloeckler

SEGMENT ROTATION SEAT

Segment Rotation Seat is a kinetic, expandable, and contractible sculptural piece of furniture. Growth and transformation are the primary conceptual ingredients.

Each rotation segment is a fluid spatial volume consisting of five plywood layers and a ratcheting system that allows a rotating core to lock in at ten different positions. Joining multiple segments creates a sitting surface.

Segment contours were determined by ergonomic study and conform to human proportions. A person can sit forward, backward, or sideways and ratchet the wood segments to positions that provide armrests, legrests, backrest, headrest, etc.

Segment Rotation Seat, 2005 | Birch-veneer plywood, stainless steel, threaded rod | 15 x 30 x 20 in.

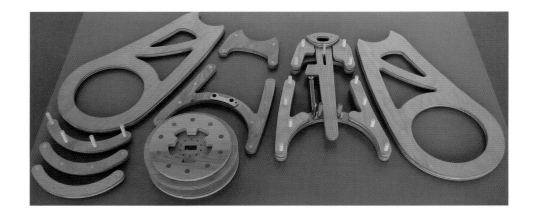

The coupler is used to connect rotation segment cores and properly space each segment. A threaded rod mechanically fastens the entire assembly.

One rotation segment is shown dissected to allow for close inspection of design, materials, assembly, structure, and mechanics. This project obviously employs CNC router technology, and no attempt was made to disguise that process. Instead, my goal was to embrace the CNC technology, but assemble the two-dimensional cut plywood plates to create something fluid and spatial. Waste is often an issue with CNC router technology, but the creation of an efficient layout of shapes on the four-by-eight-foot sheet of plywood factored into the design process at an early stage, resulting in remarkable efficiency.

Whimsy is often a fundamental element in my work. I would hope that a person's first reaction to *Segment Rotation Seat* might be humor, followed very closely by curiosity and a great desire to explore and interact with the assembly. The idea of sitting, and comfort, is the result of thorough experimentation and frequent adjustment. Sitting becomes active instead of passive. The inevitable consequence of interaction with *Segment Rotation Seat* is a unique understanding of human motion and body mechanics.

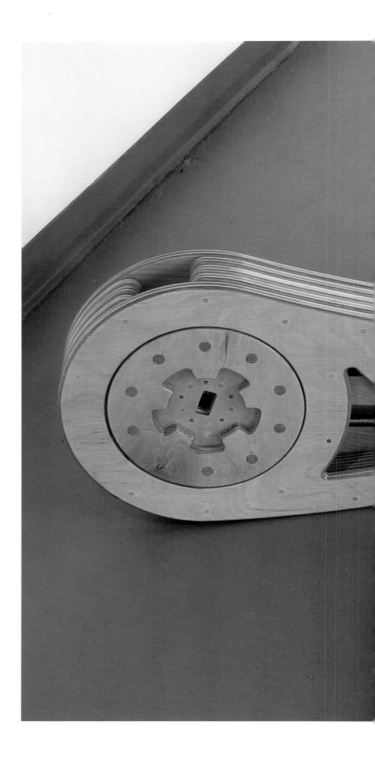

Doug Jones & Carrie Compton

THE NINTH CHAIR: BEYOND BURNT

Through experimentation with fire and wood and various finishes, we became inspired by the changes in the characteristics of wood that emerged in the burning process, especially the effects on end grain. We were particularly struck by the beauty of white oak and the emergence of the cellular structure/growth rings that appeared when the cellulose burned and was scrubbed away and the durable lignin remained. Transformations in color, texture, technical properties, and working abilities were explored through a repeated process of burning, scouring away the charred cellulose, applying liming wax, and rubbing out.

Throughout our process and experimentation we were pleased and surprised to discover the extent to which our process was controllable or uncontrollable. For instance, some edges of the chair frame developed their own organic and imperfect shaping and the wax on the seat and back was a bit more malleable than expected. We were able to control and highlight a bit more of the natural coloration in the white oak (bringing out more browns) versus the black and white that originally appeared with the application of white wax.

The Ninth Chair: Beyond Burnt, 2015 | Alder, white oak, wax | 40 x 20 x 21 in. | Margot Geist, Geistlight Photography

Designing and building this piece was not limited to a collaborative interplay of ideas, experimentation, and design viewpoint but also, we realized, it was a collaboration between wood and fire. The simple unadorned chair frame became the canvas for a blend between structure and the organic as the alder frame's once-crisp lines softened in the burning process, showcasing the temper of fire on wood; the wood's own imperfections blending seamlessly with the refined grace of fine woodworking. The alder's light tones turned a particularly rich color after the charred blackness was rubbed away, and unique organic edges became apparent depending on where the fire caught or burned more deeply. The panels of white oak end grain that make up the seat and back were texturized and softened as well, helping to integrate them with the form of the frame.

This project was a successful blend of the technical and intuitive natures of woodworking using common species in unexpected and unconventional ways, to be experienced against a backdrop of a simple chair form. The elemental "treeness" of growth rings transformed into a refined seat with a strong

visual and textural statement. Gridlines appeared along the glued end grain of the panels as flame dried and scoured the surface, creating an overlaid pattern that enhances the natural geometry and characteristics of wood. The pattern and texture of wood replaces the pattern and texture of a more traditional upholstered back and seat. We feel that the twenty-first century will be about making the most of precious limited resources and that creatively approaching common woods and materials leads to good, sustainable design. We hope that a sitter will be intrigued by the surfaces and processes represented in this chair and be inspired that common woods can be transformed by thoughtful design.

Lauren Kalman

BUT IF THE CRIME IS BEAUTIFUL ...
COMPOSITION WITH ORNAMENT AND OBJECT

But if the Crime Is Beautiful ... Composition with Ornament and Object (18), 2014 | Inkjet print | 20 x 16 in.

My work combines functional and craft objects, sculpture, photography, video, installation, and performance. Through my work, I bring to light uncomfortable connections in visual culture between body image, media, class, and style.

My recent body of work, *But if the Crime Is Beautiful,* utilizes a sterile aesthetic borrowed from modernism combined with adornment and the female body. Fabricated objects that reflect sculptural ornamentation and adornment are combined with the body and furniture to produce photographs. This work is instigated by the architect Adolf Loos's 1910 lecture *"Ornament and Crime."* Loos proposes that ornament is regressive and that in contemporary society, only degenerates are decorated (this includes women). Loos's writings on architecture and design helped to define the principles of the modern design movement. The influence of modernism permeates the contemporary built environment and therefore impacts our psychological and bodily relationship to space and objects. The "crime" in my work points not only to the decorated, but also to female sexuality.

The furniture in *But if the Crime Is Beautiful* represents this modernist lineage. The figures and fabricated objects, positioned on or around the furniture and architecture, point to a variety of historical, political, and social contexts relating to religious iconography, sex, gender, power, pleasure, and torture. Many of the objects, in contrast to modernist furniture, reference decorative medieval and Renaissance sculptural renditions of celestial, ephemeral, or otherworldly forms, like clouds, sunbeams, smoke, and halos.

The work also explores the elevation of modern design to status items (aligning the owner with the taste level of an elite class) through combining modern design with gold and gilding. Gilding plays upon constructions of taste, and in my work, references excess. I use the modern design as a symbol of restraint and intellectual control.

In the selected images there is a stark contrast between the lightness of the figures and the background and the starkness of the dark laminated wood. There is a confounding of the function of the chair because the bodies rest on the furniture in ways that they were not intended to and are a forceful interruption to the iconic status of the chairs. There is, however, still a visual harmony between the bodies, objects, and chairs: with the legs and backs of the chairs mirroring or repeating the forms of the bodies and props, and through a continuation of the contour edges of the bodies and objects.

But if the Crime Is Beautiful is a multimedia project composed of images, objects, and sculpture, with series subtitled *Composition with Ornament and Object, Hoods, A/tared, Sculptures/Reliquaries,* and *Monstrance.* In total it includes approximately fifty photographs and twenty objects/sculptures.

Patrick Kana

INCREMENTUM

Mankind's fascination with natural form is undeniably long-lived. From collecting and preserving specimens for evolutionary research, to documenting and expressing natural form through artistic practice, mankind continues to embrace for scientific and aesthetic benefit that which surrounds us. I believe that botany, marine biology, and environmental phenomena—all areas of influence and study from my childhood—are sources that illustrate perfection in form and utility. The sheer beauty evident in these scientific forms continues to inspire me, and I celebrate them and explore my relationship with them through an experimental making process in wood.

By selecting specific examples from my past involvement with the sciences, I aim to convey a sense of pure wonder with my interpretation of natural form in my bench *Incrementum*. I arrived at this form through the examination of specific curved wood samples that I myself had collected, with the intention of establishing a conversation between the design process and the material. I respond to wood's tactility, its preciousness, its origin, and its identity, and I feel a responsibility to honor the medium. The material for *Incrementum*, named after its suggested flow or growth as a botanical or biological tendril, was selected for its naturally grown curves and gesture. By embracing the curves that were provided to me by the tree, I was able to reveal an inherent gesture of the material while simultaneously introducing my own visual vocabulary of interpreted botanical form.

Incrementum, 2015 |
Soft maple, limestone |
72 x 16 x 13 in. | Elizabeth
Torgerson-Lamark

Rather than reproduce life-forms, I apply my particular knowledge of and fascination with the natural world to explore the process of designing and making objects and furniture in wood. Form exploration and experimentation is of utmost importance in my current research and practice, not utility, although I use the context of furniture to help ground me in my development. Ultimately, my goal with creating the bench *Incrementum* was to provide the viewer and user a stimulating experience upon which they can ponder the natural world, perhaps their natural world, and engage in a tactile experience similar to exploring found specimens that capture the eye in the wild. Ultimately, I am aiming to establish a working process that feels seamless and fluid between the material, the inspiration, and my hand.

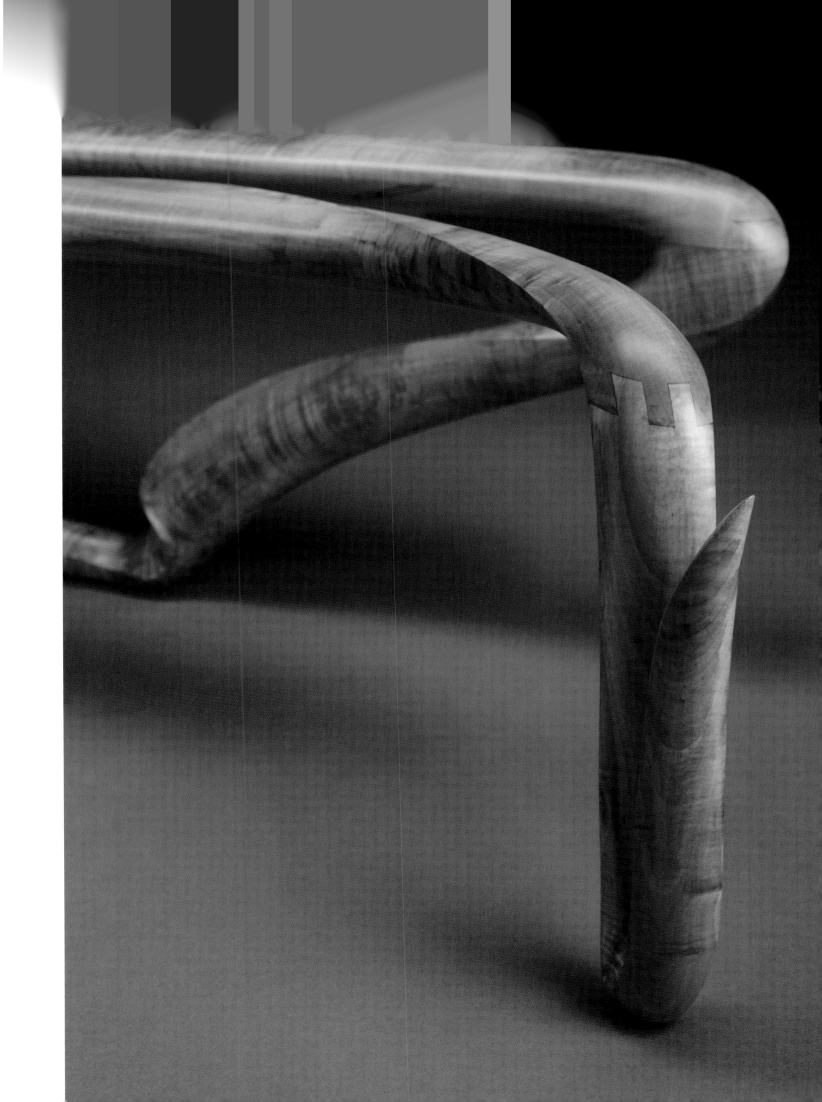

David Knopp

CHAIR

I have explored the aesthetic qualities of line for many years, first with life drawings, then with sculpture. A single line can express gesture and movement, direction and depth on a flat surface. With my first sculptures using plywood, I was surprised to discover the linear strata inherent in the medium. Carving laminated blocks of plywood, I create flowing, liquid lines that engage the senses as the eye travels over the contours of my objects. I prefer an intuitive process, viewing collaboration between ideas and materials as central to my creative output.

My creations start with a vision and a rudimentary sketch. There are no defined templates or 3-D models or software used. My pieces are functional, but I tend to focus on the aesthetic qualities rather than design principles. Every finished piece is one of a kind. The constant changes that occur as I work keep the work alive as it morphs into my interpretation. The process is paramount. In my work I never know, nor do I try to guess, the end result. I have the freedom to experience and flow with the work. I can feel how it fits in an architectural space as I build. Yet I can push limits of balance and size, forgetting traditional furniture standards. I choose to keep in mind the concept of functionality. For some reason, I need to justify four to six months' worth of work by creating something useful but also beautiful and pleasing.

My technique is difficult to describe in words. But being hands-on is central. When working on a piece to be used as seating, I put my body into the work. I constantly walk around the piece, sit in it, feeling the curves as I get into

Chair, 2015 | Baltic birch, plywood | 32 x 60 x 36 in.

final carving. I let my body be my guide. This helps assure it will be a comfortable experience for the user. Hopefully they are lured to relax as their bodies conform to the contours.

The unknown factor is what my work is about. It often barely resembles the initial sketch or anything I may have had in mind. The piece always unconsciously gets in my head and changes, both in my vision of it and then in

actuality. That is why it seems that sometimes the work occurs outside of me and I may not know how I got there. It takes over.

Chair is a work in progress that is close to completion—with some additional refining of contours, sanding, and final coats of finish, it will be ready to exhibit. Any doubts that come to my mind after months of labor and interaction are erased with the words, "I want to sit in it."

Beth Krensky

PORTABLE SANCTUARY #1

Change—effecting it personally and socially—is very important to me. My artistic practice dwells within a living paradigm. One that supports the life and sustainability of the individual, the planet, and "lives" as a flexible entity that can change and respond to different contexts and ideas.

Portable Sanctuary #1, complete with leather straps—and with Psalm 23 engraved on the seat of an old classroom chair made of oak—is intended to be "wandered" or carried on one's back, much like a backpack. To perform it, I have fitted it on my own back and carried it through the forest. As I'm walking, whenever I'm ready, I put it down and sit on it, and when I see fit, I take it up again.

The psalm reads, "The Lord is my shepherd, I shall not want … he maketh me to lie down in green pastures …" and, not surprisingly, I feel the work as a whole resonates best when activated in a pastoral setting, far away from human presence. Breeze, sunlight; and the individual/wearer sitting with a sense of intention and comfort.

Portable Sanctuary #1, Performance Video, 2012 | Video | Josh Blumental

Joseph G. La Macchia

CONTINUUM CHAIR & CONTINUUM TABLE: SITTING STOOL

All of my work starts in one of two places: from the form itself, or the wood that becomes its shape. The Continuum Collection was born from the wood. In this instance, from a locally salvaged urban walnut tree that I air-dried for three years while I waited—as I always do—for the exact right idea to come along.

Unlike most of my ideas, this was not a flash of inspiration in the middle of the night, nor was it the result of exhaustive experimentation. Rather, the *Continuum Chair* and *Continuum Table: Sitting Stool* were the inevitable outgrowth of a series of creative events in my life that began midway through 2012—my first year providing for my family solely as a furniture maker—and culminated near the end of 2013 with a shift toward table work that produced a new console table design that became the first piece in the Continuum Collection.

The console table received one of the three Best in Show awards for the *Urban Wood Encounter* exhibit at Design Within Reach and was published in the Milwaukee Journal Sentinel's *Lake Country* magazine. The piece received such interest and provoked such intrigue by booth visitors at the One of a Kind Show in Chicago that in early 2014 I was inspired to create a larger desk based on the design.

Naturally, after building the desk, my attention moved toward building a complementary chair. At first my interest was purely functional (you can't have a desk without a chair, after all), but as the build progressed it became clear that the chair was meant to stand more freely on its own, while remaining

Continuum Chair,
2014 | Urban walnut |
30 x 22 x 24 in.

Continuum Table: Sitting Stool, 2014 | Urban walnut | 20 x 16 in.

connected to the desk and the console table by common design elements that would come to define the Continuum Collection—paired legs, waterfall and book-matched grain, pillowed bridle joints, and the same source tree.

Of course, as a furniture line maker, once you have a freestanding chair, now you need a side table. But what if you could create something that was more than just an accent table? Something that was even more functional. That is when the *Continuum Chair* and *Continuum Table: Sitting Stool* blossomed in my mind's eye. It combines the paired leg design and pillowed bridled joints of the chair and features a unique center hub as an anchor point for the buttressed legs that share the same angle as the chair's single back legrest. It is the perfect complement to the *Continuum Chair*.

Some pieces come together so quickly and easily it's as though they built themselves, and we as makers are merely the vessels these pieces pass through on their path to creation. Other pieces demand more of their craftsman; they ask us to question each decision as they take shape and come to life. These works are a collaborative journey between the idea, the medium, the piece being born, and the hands that bring it to life. The latter was the case with the *Continuum Chair*; the former with the *Continuum Table: Sitting Stool*. One demanded more of me than any piece I had built to date, the other merely asked me to stay out of its way as it emerged from the locally salvaged urban walnut tree whose purpose I'd been waiting to discover for nearly three years.

Jack Larimore

RE-PAIR

I made this piece while in residency at the Oregon College of Art and Craft in 2008.

The more I thought about Oregon, the more I focused on an interesting contradiction particular to this region that relates to my work. The Northwest is a mecca for contemporary alternative lifestyle while having a long history of clear-cut logging and commercial timber production that's been pretty tough on the environment and habitats. The new Portland was familial to me; the old Portland was somewhat tricky. The romance of timbering is chilled by the realities of the clear-cut. In the presence of an old-growth Douglas fir, a two-by-four takes on a different value. My affinity for wood as a medium is invigorated by the life that a tree represents; logging, then, is an inconvenient truth that I don't often confront.

During the OCAC residency I came to the realization that my interest in salvaged timber may simply be a part of a larger cultural need to find some sense of reparation through reusing, recycling, reclaiming. We are a consuming culture and it is less embarrassing if we, in some small way, reuse, recycle, and reclaim. This piece is the result of my two-week residency spent exploring reparation as intent. Happily, I found that there exists a sensuous relationship between an old log and an old timber.

re-pair, 2008 |
Douglas fir |
52 x 68 x 32 in.

This application has renewed my interest in the revelations that this piece brought me. Over the course of the next twelve months, I intend to site these chairs at a number of locations and on them conduct conversations about trees, lumber, sustainable consumption, and incremental concentric growth with the intent of publishing a journal that reports and illustrates these conversations.

Po Shun Leong

FORTUNE COOKIE STOOL

When the wood stool popped out of the sun-heated bending mold, it looked like a giant fortune cookie.

If there was a (booby) prize for the most misused design cliché, a firm favorite would be "form follows function," with "less is more" coming a close second.

Not only is "form follows ..." often quoted incorrectly, it is not even accurate: the original wording was "form ever follows function." It is also routinely misattributed, mostly to twentieth-century modernist grandees like Le Corbusier and Mies van der Rohe, but was actually coined by the less famous American architect Louis Sullivan.[1]

The *Fortune Cookie Stool* exists because "function follows form," not "form follows function."

PAPER MODELS

Since the 1970s, I have experimented with small abstract paper models without any particular end use except that a few of the shapes might have suggested a function. I free my mind from preconceived notions of what the cardboard shape is finally supposed to become, and instead let it be an open-ended playdate with scissors, cardboard, and tape that could lead to the unexpected inspiration to what it might become.

Fortune Cookie Stool,
2008 | Bent laminated polywood, paint |
18½ x 19 x 18 in.

NOTE

1.   Alice Rawsthorn, "The Demise of 'Form Follows Function,'" *The New York Times,* May 30, 2009.

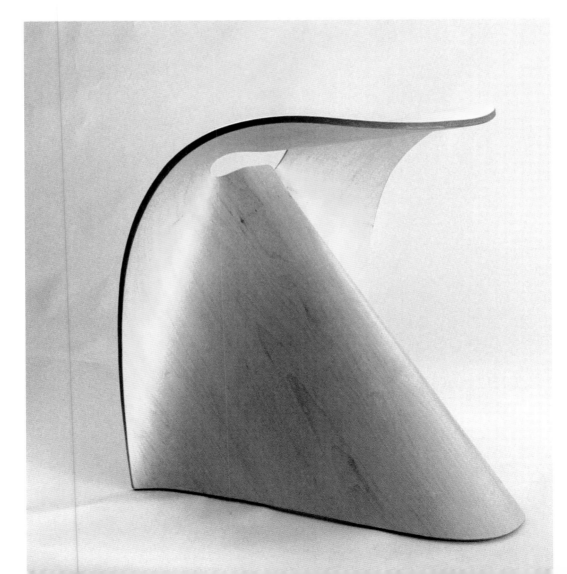

Laura Mays

AMPLE

For several years I have been exploring chair forms that create places in themselves, as well as support for the body—places of rest, refuge, shelter, and ease. Their precedent is the high-backed porters' chairs that sat in the cold hallways of large houses in the British Isles, as well as wingback chairs, which traditionally faced a fire and rose high enough behind the sitter's head to protect from drafts. The chairs are almost architectural themselves in their formation of space and place.

These chairs make many allusions—to natural objects such as shells or pods, and to manufactured objects—a vessel, a cradle, a coffin, a barrel. The most recent of these explorations is the chair I am submitting: *Ample*. It is made from American ash, cut into curved staves from ¾ material, creating a stripiness in the quartered grain. The sides of the chair are compound curved: like a barrel they curve in the up and down direction as well as from front to back to form a sort of voluptuous protected space, which is upholstered in a striped velvet material. The chair is wide and low, accommodating a variety of postures within it beyond the traditional. The stand is straightforward and made from narra.

I believe that the manner in which an object is made contributes to its meaning. In this case the process is straightforward and apparent in the finished piece. It requires no knowledge of woodworking processes to apprehend how it was made. There is pleasure in the repetition and rhythm of the staves, how the many become one. The sides were shaped by hand, using spokeshaves and scrapers, and thus are marginally asymmetrical (not noticeably so, I hope).

Ample, 2015 |
Ash, narra, upholstery |
46 x 28 x 32 in.

It is one of the paradoxes of craft that a craftsperson attempts to use as much skill, care, time, and attention as necessary to get the work right—in this case, symmetry—and yet one of the values of craft is an indication of the humanity of the maker, their fallibility and inability to attain perfection. And so I relish that paradox, striving to do my best but acknowledging that I will never attain any form of perfection. The back is a panel, veneered in European ash, which is slightly lighter and more yellow in tone than the American ash. The ash components are finished with shellac.

My intention is that someone sitting in this chair feels protected and sheltered; that they can find a comfortable position that supports their body; that if they let their hands sweep the inside or the outside, they feel the bulge and smooth swell of the sides. It is a chair for interiority and reflection within oneself.

Christine Mei

SHAPESHIFTER

To invent a successful chair is one of design's most extreme challenges. What causes this process to be tremendously tough? Each piece of the chair has to serve a structural or tangible purpose. Every element has to be ergonomic yet seemingly beautiful. This was the start of my chair, *Shapeshifter*.

I approached the chair with three tedious steps: discovery, design, and development. During the discovery stage, my mind became a sponge, absorbing every detail of assorted seats. I was conducting general research of chairs in different showrooms throughout Manhattan. Some questions were: What are the dimensions of the chairs? Where are the pressure points? How beneficial are the joints? What are the materials and finishes? Who are the targeted users? What are the emotional responses? How much is each chair? Who designed them?

This phase reminds me of the saying, "When you're lost, you take everything in." As a designer, I use my observations to acquire new insight—despite my previous familiarity with chairs. After gaining more knowledge, I designed with my intuition from there.

The early inspiration behind *Shapeshifter* was constant madness, because the design possibilities were endless. It then occurred to me that my chair should be adaptable to the user's needs as well as being

Shapeshifter, 2015 |
Plywood | 30 x 30 x 20 in.

strong and durable for various sitting conditions. As I was sketching, I noticed a piece of string on the floor. It looped around itself like the shape of a cancer awareness ribbon. It led me to think, "What if this line could be the side view of my chair?" I played around with the shape, drawing numerous ideations while rotating the form.

When I drafted a full-scale version of my chair, the design became finalized. It is finally ergonomic throughout each of the four sitting positions as a lounge, dining, armrest, and rocking chair. *Shapeshifter* is basically a four-in-one chair. The user can simply rotate my chair from one position to the next for different benefits. The lounge position extends the user's body to relax effortlessly. The dining position directs the user's lower back to sit up straight for a healthier spine; this position could also be used as an office chair. The armrest position allows the user to sit sideways, since the other positions require the user to sit parallel with my chair. Lastly, the rocking position offers the ability to sway back and forth while sitting, in case the user is bored, needs to exercise, or wants to release his or her anxiety.

Constructed entirely out of plywood, the material of my chair is reduced to a simple yet expressive form.

Each speck of *Shapeshifter* was carefully thought out—even with the daunting constraints of ergonomic regulations and high expectations from potential users. From wanting to create an original chair that has a curvy and thin character, I have accomplished *Shapeshifter*—a chair that has an attitude of being captivating, inviting, relaxing, and timeless. The experience of sitting down on *Shapeshifter* should offer freedom with precision. It should promise complexity with direct delivery. It should be felt as wonder with relief.

Ultimately, a successful chair must be magic with scientific underpinnings. From discovering, designing, and developing *Shapeshifter*, I imagine that users now have the opportunity to sit differently from one chair. Furthermore, the meaning of a chair has been refined for me. Through researching, a chair is described as a seat with a back. Through designing, a chair is designated to have an ergonomic seat and a back. Through constructing, a chair is defined as a well-developed idea of an ergonomic seat and a back with unlimited potential.

Taiji Miyasaka

SKINNY LOVE CHAIR

The inspiration for the design of the *Skinny Love Chair* is based on two questions: "How can I design a chair that looks ordinary but also inspiring?" and "How can a chair design be true to a material (wood)?"

To respond to the first question, a simple and smooth form was designed for the side elevation of the chair. Instead of trying to come up with an eye-catching form, my design seeks to fit in multiple contexts. For this purpose, I looked at various types of chairs in my surroundings and checked their dimensions in relation to the human body. My design is an abstraction of ordinary commonalities among these chairs.

Skinny Love Chair, 2011 |
Oak | 32 x 16¾ x 18½ in.

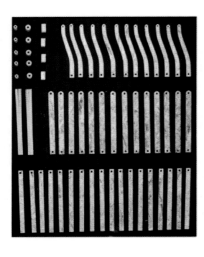

In answer to the second question, initially, plywood and OSB were selected as materials whose characteristics might inform the chair designs. Plywood forms linear and planar elements to create a chair, and OSB sheets are cut into shape and compiled longitudinally to compose the chair design. In the final design for the *Skinny Love* Chair, I used ⅛"-thick oak wood strips and oak wood blocks to articulate the chair design. This design is informed by the elasticity and lightness of the wood, but the elevation and approximate dimensions of the chair are the same as those made from plywood and OSB. As a result, a space was carefully crafted between two pieces of wood, and this was repeated as a unit horizontally and vertically to form the chair (this page). The final design of the chair may have a flat surface as a seating area.

The options are presented in one of the digital images. I am hoping that those who sit on the *Skinny Love Chair* enjoy the marriage of the thinness of the wood strips and the light structure created by assembling the wood strips. The design of this chair allows it to blend into various scenes in an unobtrusive manner.

Mira Nakashima

CONCORDIA CHAIR

The *Concordia Chair*, originally designed on the back of a music program in 2003, was named for the Concordia Chamber Players whose live concerts first drove the inspiration. On observing their vigorous, volatile, expressive, full-body playing style, I thought they should have some chairs that were of comparable quality to the music they were playing. Initially, I offered to loan a set of George Nakashima *New Chairs* (1955), which they graciously accepted only to discover their needs as musicians differed greatly from those of a casually dining household. With this, I offered to design and produce an entirely new chair. Their leader, Michelle Djokic, requested the seating have no arms to interfere with their bowing, that they have flat seats so they could move freely about as they related musically to each other, and that they should be exactly 17.5″ from the floor. Her generosity in insight went as far as offering an English walnut tree that was being removed from her family home in New Hope, so the first set of seven was made primarily from this beautiful tree.

I thought it would be important to shape the chair with the two front corners supported fully by sturdy legs, and that there should be some minimal back support for the musicians to briefly lean on during occasional pauses in the music. As the back of the seat did not need to be as wide as the front, the shape became a free-form triangle, opposite in orientation from my father's *Mira Chair* design from the 1950s. Paring down the crest rail of my father's *Conoid Chair* from 1960, a minimal crest rail emerged, perched on the single back leg support and locked in with a through-tenon. Unlike the previous

Concordia Chair, 2003 | **American black walnut** | 31½ x 19½ x 16 in.

Concordia Chair — in Context, 2013 | Black walnut and East Indian rosewood | 30–44 x 18 x 18 in.

Nakashima chairs, the *Concordia* has no spindles reminiscent of the Windsor-style chairs my father designed and made, but is more sculptural and akin to some of the Danish-designed chairs of the twentieth century.

My dear cellist friend Michelle was happy they performed well onstage but suggested adding a small cushion to prevent their costumes from "squeaking" as they moved around on the wood! My assistant designer, Miriam Carpenter, solved this secondary design challenge quite gracefully; we chose a beautiful Thai silk for the cushion covers and designed a discreet Velcro fastening to hold the divided strap ends together. However, as we aim to choose highly figured wood for these sculptural chair seats, we recommend leaving it exposed to show off the grain. As with all Nakashima chairs, the finish is hand-rubbed tung oil, which deepens and mellows with age.

We hope that users of the Concordia Chair will enjoy its simplicity, sturdiness, and lyricism, as well as appreciate the joinery, craftsmanship, and unique patterns of the wood grain. Chairs are among the more difficult design challenges, as they must fit human form and function as well as be structurally sound and pleasing to the eye. Thank you, Concordia, for the inspiration!

Christy Oates

FACET CHAIR

My folding furniture is made for living in small spaces. The idea is that less is more, and the furniture is made using eco-friendly materials and cutting processes. These flat-pack wall-mounted furniture pieces are inspired by origami forms. Laser cutting provides the benefit of negligible material waste; the cutoffs between the furniture shapes are used within the wall mount, conserving material and creating a piece of functional wall art.

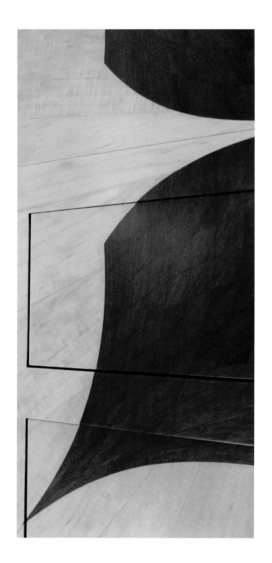

Facet Chair, 2012 | Plywood, maple and sapele wood veneers | 16 x 16 x 33 in.

Keunho Peter Park

COCOON CHAIR

I believe smooth wooden surfaces that allow for direct body contact, such as a chair, bench, or even stair railing, provide a sensory experience with enjoyment and warmth. This kind of distinctly human interaction naturally leads me to associate wood with human skin. My goal is for the audience to touch, feel, and sit on the piece so that the interaction creates an intimate experience with the object.

The forms that I create with wood also relate to my interest in the beauty of the human body and the significance of human musculature. I continue to research various innovative ways of creating organic free forms that not only complement wood but also incorporate structural integrity and practicality.

Cocoon Chair, 2013 | Cherry | 59 x 72 x 156 in.

Gord Peteran

ELECTRIC CHAIR

Marcel Breuer pushed the limits of new structural technology. He also pushed the limits of trust *normally associated* with a chair. Surely, this would fail them ... and hurt them.

I have restored his devious line with another human paranoia: electrocution.

Electric Chair, 2006 |
Metal, bulb |
36 x 14 x 18 in.

Dean Pulver

MEMORIAL BENCH

In 2008 I was fortunate enough to have the experience of a residency at the Center for Furniture Craftsmanship in Rockport, Maine. I was interested in exploring some new directions with my work and hoped the experience would help me do so. One of my focuses was to strip things down to their bare essence; to eliminate anything that did not support the intent of the piece.

The surroundings became clues and inspirations for forms, spaces, and atmospheres. Coming from the Taos, New Mexico, desert, I found the ocean, boats, and their relationship to land and space stood out in my mind because of their familiarity and differences from my usual landscape. Various things started to strike me, such as the masts on boats and how they mark a place and space but also aim and lead up to the skies; how boats become resting spaces in the void of water; how the boat buoys begin to define spaces in the vast ocean. At the same time, working in a studio with other makers who were generally more interested in traditional forms of furniture making made me want to oppose that very format. I wanted to speak of things beyond the form of the piece; decoration was not what I was interested in.

I had a lot of reflective time since I was away from my usual business duties and routines. I was thinking about our existence on this planet and the passing of people's lives, and how an empty space is left when they are gone and how their memories live on in our minds. How would I best represent these thoughts? How could I mark the mental space that they exist in and from which they transition onward? I wanted both an object to reflect upon and also a place and space to be in to do so. This *Memorial Bench* is that answer for me.

Memorial Bench, 2008 |
Bleached ash |
110 x 58 x 58 in.

My hope is that the experience of this piece would be a reflective one; silent yet thoughtful. It's not my character to preach or dictate to people, so therefore I'm not interested in one-liners or defined statements, I'm interested in objects that resonate through reference. Reference to objects and memories in our lives and experiences that had an impact on us and have left an imprint. Maybe something primal, maybe something recent, but something that touched us deeply and memorably. Maybe these relationships are understandable or maybe not; that is not important. What is important is the moment of silent reflection that I hope to bring about.

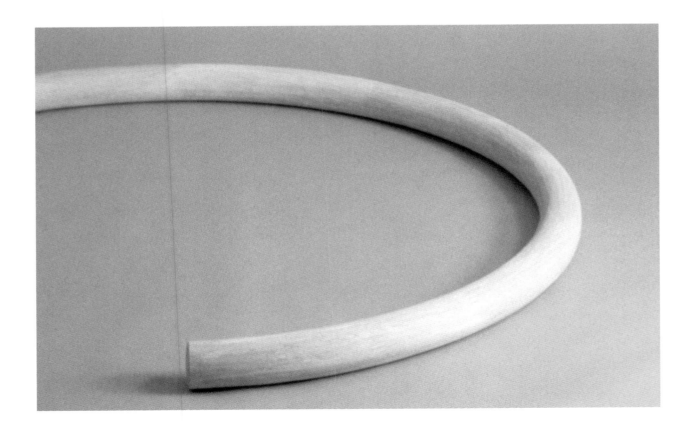

Andrew Jay Rumpler

TATUM'S LOUNGE

Tatum's Lounge is a project that explores the structural limits of a found group of parts, all similar but none the same, in the creation of a chair dedicated to the wonderful stride pianist Arthur Tatum.

Deemed "the greatest pianist in any style" by Sergei Rachmaninoff, Art Tatum was a man of immeasurable talent who created sounds both wonderful and chaotic. Made up of twenty-five salvaged piano keys (and very little else), *Tatum's Lounge* was built over the course of two years in an organic manner something like a Tatum piano solo: with both order and abandon.

As in Tatum's playing where there is the perception of structure—an identifiable melody, a dependable time signature—there are also things about *Tatum's Lounge* that might give one pause. The seat, which is mostly a translucent skin, inspires little trust, as frequent and sudden key changes in the pianist's playing might cause some uneasiness. Part of the listening, then, involves a suspension of disbelief in order to enjoy what one cannot immediately make sense of. The word *lounge* in the title refers to both a style of chair and the physical spaces in which a pianist of the 1940s, like Tatum, would have played. The Lenox Lounge in Harlem exists to this day as an example.

Tatum's Lounge, 2010 |
Recycled piano keys, resin and glass fiber, steel |
29½ x 18½ x 23 in.

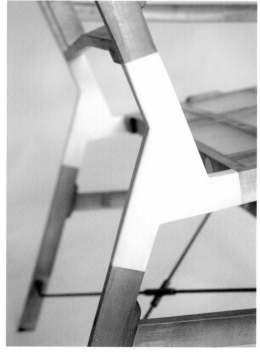

Weighing just six pounds but the size of an average chair (and functional—it can be sat in), *Tatum's Lounge* seems an impossibility. A lattice of angled pieces, some crossing, others terminating, give little hint at what binds them. In fact what cannot be seen is what provides the chair's strength: a small mortise and tenon at each intersection, thirty-six in all. *Tatum's Lounge,* one could say, asks of its occupant some of the same commitment as the great pianist's music asks of its listeners: a certain amount of trust before delivering its reward.

Fabiano Sarra

SPADA CHAIR

I think of my work as being driven by a constant pursuit of the "perfect form." I strive to design objects that are simple in nature; objects whose complexity lies in their details. I approach my designs from all sides through a process of refinement that starts with a simple sketch and ends with a functional object. This process is one that is carried over from design to design as my work evolves, starting every new project with the thought of how I could improve the last.

It is purely an expression of my personal aesthetic. I work toward a deep understanding of each piece I design so that every step I take in building can be carefully planned and executed. Construction of my work is about process since I primarily employ traditional woodworking techniques, but often my work will also involve the use of digital fabrication. When designing a new object, I think about the overall form and how it will stand against the test of time. I try to design pieces that exhibit the quality of my materials and quietly flaunt their elegance. My goal is to design objects that exhibit iconic qualities and have the potential for establishing themselves in any environment.

Spada Chair, 2012 | Ebonized ash, white oak, brass | 24 x 22 x 18 in.

Matt
Selnick

STROBO

The Planar Chair is the final project of Year 1 in the industrial design program at Philadelphia University. Students learn to manage the relationship of planar shapes in three-dimensional space through this exercise.

Work begins with the creation of abstract planar form studies, followed by a broad firsthand survey of multiple seating styles—from task chairs to lounge seating—to understand the strengths and weaknesses of each. At the same time, broad-based three-dimensional exploration begins as a large number of scale models are created.

For our final project of our Design 2 semester, I wanted to create a planar chair that accentuated something visual, rather than just create an interesting form. As my design process developed, I began to look for the aspect that my design needed. For this, I incorporated the photographic effect of displaying motion through multiple frames, also known as the stroboscopic, or sequence, effect. Portraying motion in the design of an object like a chair seemed like a challenge that I wanted to pursue. A chair is static; it does not move, it stays in the same place for extended periods of time, and you use it for sitting. There is no general motion involved in a chair. I found that creating a chair that gives the sense of motion and visually produces an effect that defines motion on a relatively fixed object was not only fun, but it was a great journey into giving my design a greater meaning and visual interpretation.

Strobo, 2015 |
Taskboard, primer, paint |
5½ x 2¾ x 4¼ in.

While I was researching chairs, I kept in mind the type of chair I wanted to design and benchmarks I wanted to hit. I did know that I wanted the chair to be ideal for a guest in a living room, in a small public space, or as a comfortable, productive chair for working on a laptop or meetings, but also for a casual household environment. These benchmarks were kept in mind throughout the design process.

My chair is ideal for being a conversational, yet productive, chair for an indoor environment. It could be used in a more formal gathering room context, or as a guest chair in a family living room. The stroboscopic effect produced would be best achieved in a very open and bright living room or sunroom. Regardless, the effect is pronounced and visible from any angle and provides a great display of shadow and motion with the negative space and planar form that it presents.

Mark Sfirri

PALLY LUDIE

CHUBBETTE

LADY WHISTLE

In my research on the woodworker Wharton Esherick, I came across a number of carved animal forms that he made for his grandson in the early 1960s. Most of them were small, but one, a stylized horse that also served as a small bench, got me thinking about making furniture out of one piece of wood as opposed to constructing it, which is my usual approach. The first hurdle was to find wood of sufficient size. I located a large pine beam (11″ x 14″) that was part of a two-hundred-year-old barn from central Pennsylvania. Then I made rough drawings of possible designs, from which I developed a series of horizontal and vertical small-scale models, or three-dimensional sketches, as I like to call them. They are lathe turnings that also have been carved. I find it easier to determine form more fully by actually making it three-dimensionally.

In *Pally Ludie*, one of the vertical stools, I wanted to create an illusion of a melon form with a half sphere on top of it to create the seat. In *Lady Whistle*, another vertical stool, I used similar shaping details but came up with an asymmetrical solution. The titles refer to an old Scandinavian children's toe-naming game (from small to large, they are: Petey Petey, Pally Ludie, Lady Whistle, Lodie Whostle, and the Great Ottomandod [with much variation on the words and spelling]).

Pally Ludie, 2014 |
White pine |
16½ x 10¾ x 10¾ in.

Chubbette, 2014 |
White pine |
13½ x 36 x 10½ in.

Lady Whistle, 2015 |
White pine |
18 x 11 x 11 in.

Chubbette, one of the horizontal stools, is a single-axis turning that provided challenges due to its size and uneven weight distribution during turning. It was subsequently hand carved while still on the lathe. *Chubbette,* along with a second piece titled *Husky Low Rider,* were named after a clothing category that was around in the 1950s and 1960s: *Chubbette* for girls, *Husky* for boys. I was discussing the title of *Husky* (having lived that life myself) with a woman who lived the life, as a girl, of a *Chubbette.* The titles seemed to fit.

I've used deciduous hardwoods exclusively all these years and looked down my nose at pine. My attitude toward it has completely changed. Pine is so easy to carve and turn that it has become one of my favorite woods. After six months or so, it turns to a warm golden color. Quite appealing.

Michaela Crie Stone

SEATED SPRINGBOK
GIGI CHAIR

I create pieces that push the parameters of function by placing value on sculptural creativity and the transformation of space, while maintaining the importance of quality craftsmanship. I believe that functional craft and discursive fine art do not have to be mutually exclusive. My objective is to create work that conveys that craft does not have to be devoid of conceptual examination, and that fine art can function outside of a vacuum and break down the fourth wall by engaging the audience through direct interaction.

I grew up in coastal Maine with an early affinity for life sciences, and nature has been a steadfast source of inspiration in my work. What I know about engineering, beauty, and balance, I learned from careful and sincere study of the environment. Patterns and structures in nature find their way into my work in both implicit and explicit ways, from using the proportions of a conch shell as the measurements for a table, to capturing the silhouette of birch trees in a wood piercing.

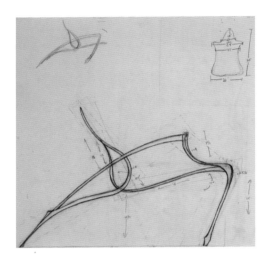

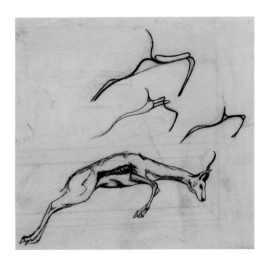

Seated Springbok, 2015 | Maple, springbok hair-on hide | 28 x 24 x 36 in. | work in progress

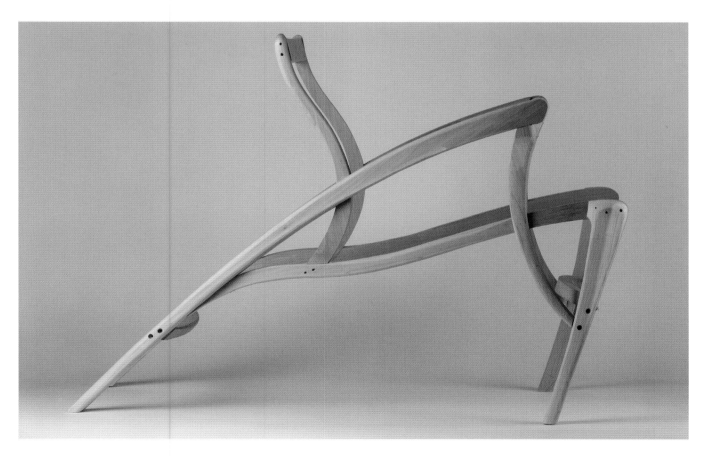

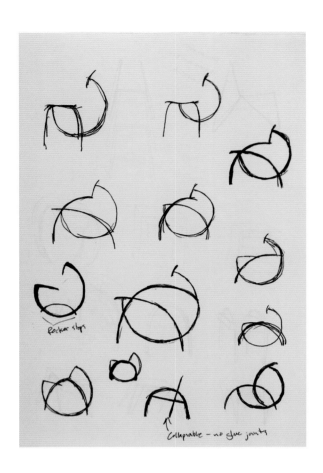

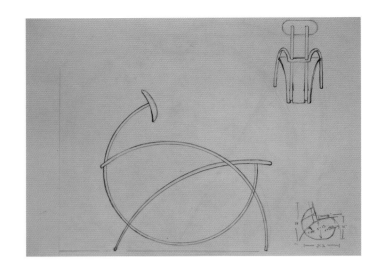

SEATED SPRINGBOK

My love of nature extends to a deep respect for animals. My mother acquired a springbok hair-on hide as a gift when she was in Africa a number of decades ago. It was subsequently given to me after many years in storage. My first reaction was reluctance. Although I am no ardent vegan, I can't help but flinch from the disrespect of treating a creature's body as a trophy. However, I realized that the best way to honor the graceful springbok that once wore the hide in front of me was to turn it into art. Thus, I have designed a sculptural chair with the silhouette of a leaping springbok, upon which the hide will act as a luxurious seat. The final piece will be made from tapered, bent laminations in maple.

GIGI CHAIR

The *Gigi Chair* is in its early stage of design. I used this chair as an expression of an unusual source of inspiration for me: typography. I've had a funny affection for typography since before I could read (I seriously used to describe the different looks of text when my mother tried to read to me), with a particular interest in the representation of the letter *G* and the ampersand symbol. In any case, a doodle in my sketchbook caught my eye as a potential chair, loosely based on the form of my favorite, seventh letter in the alphabet. This chair will be made of bent laminations in maple, along with curvilinear steel.

Gigi Chair, 2015 |
Maple, steel |
28 x 18 x 26 in.

Joshua M. Torbick

WEDGED IN

RESTRUCTURED CHAIR

Most able-bodied people engage in their daily routine unaware of the relative ease of moving through their physical environments. Standard furniture and architectural forms are designed to facilitate the comfort and productivity of typically shaped and typically equipped people in their home or work environment. However, not everybody's needs are met by these standard specifications. After losing my leg in a motorcycle accident, my awareness of this inequitable reality was sharpened considerably.

Due in part to my personal circumstance, I developed a strong interest in how physical differences preclude some individuals from fully engaging in functional and joyful activities. In pursuit of this objective, I am exploring the power inherent in furniture design to restore an individual's physical functionality, sense of independence, and fuller inclusion in meaningful work and social engagement. I draw on my own personal history and build works relevant to my experience of adaptation and acceptance.

Wedged In is an experiment in body position; I wanted to build a piece of furniture that would hold an occupant in a standing body position without using the muscles of their lower body. I looked to "executive furniture" and my prosthetic leg for design cues. Like

Wedged In, 2015 |
Walnut, steel, leather |
25 x 16 x 45 in.

a prosthetic, *Wedged In* is built with an additive construction logic: each part does its job and is connected to the next part with custom hardware. The rich walnut and soft leather, however, offers the suggestion of luxury. It is strong but flexible, very hard where it needs to be and very soft where it contacts the body.

Wedged In is built to be entered into more then sat on. It has a base, or floor, creating the sense of a place that one is almost inside of when using it. The two leather pads are set at specific angles relative to each other and the base that encourage a user to rest their shins and knees against the front while relaxing their weight against the back. Because this furniture form holds a person in a standing position without requiring the use of their legs it can truly be thought of as a prosthetic of position.

It is my hope that by addressing our physical differences and by appreciating the needs of people with lesser physical ability, the landscape of objects and architecture can be made more accommodating. My work affirms the rights of unique persons to fully realize a participatory and purposeful life.

Restructured Chair was designed and built as a complete functional piece of furniture and then subjected to a destructive action. In this case fire, a natural enemy to wood, was used to cause damage to the structural integrity of the chair without completely destroying the base material, thus removing its functionality and also setting the stage for a revival of purpose. With one leg and part of the seat surface missing there was not enough stability in the resultant form for it to be useful as furniture. With the primary structure compromised, a second structural system was used to restore the piece to function. This restructuring process returns function to the piece as furniture but requires the object to be used differently than before.

Restructured Chair, 2015 | Ash | 24 x 19 x 43 in.

Misha Volf

4 X 4 BENCH

To sit is to settle, to find oneself in a place, even if momentarily.

Whether we are seeking respite in a patio rocking chair, dominance in an executive office throne, or piety in a church pew, objects made for sitting are as much a response to the needs of our bodies as they are formative of our relationships to place.

As modern markers of identity such as nationality and ethnicity continue to dissolve, notions of place and the material structures that support them have begun to take on new meanings. Furniture, once seen as a material anchor to a localized inheritance of resources, knowledge, and history, today is often touted as "light to ship" and "easy to move"—a transient commodity in a globalized network of capital flows.

The chair, then—a hyper-local structure that engages us at the scale of the body—becomes a somewhat conflicted object. Its power to settle becomes compromised. As we work from home or jet through international airspace, the chair puts us in a place, even while that place seems to be slipping away.

This is the context in which the piece of seating furniture presented here exists. Made with construction lumber, oversized casters, and ratchet straps, the *4 x 4 Bench* was designed to move easily within a large living room: functioning as a secluded resting pad in one location, and as theater seating for film screenings in another.

Despite the convenience, these materials collude in the object to negotiate its transience. The standard 4 x 4″ structural elements are cut from eastern red

4 x 4 Bench, 2015 | Eastern red cedar, ratchet straps | 32 x 60 x 31 in.

cedar, a common construction material in the American northeast. This ubiquity, along with the species' being native to the region and the substantial mass of the material present in the object, settle the bench in its intended place. The casters, on the other hand—engineered in Germany with steel from India and blue polyurethane from China—dislocate the seat. They transport the bench away toward extended functionality, toward ease of mobility, toward a global, ever-on-the-move citizenship.

Already by the middle of the nineteenth century, material infrastructures like transport and communications were radically changing our ideas of place. Today, places are increasingly digitally enabled by, but ultimately escaping, materiality altogether. By using industrial infrastructure components in the *4 x 4 Bench*, the bench embodies the contemporary contradictions of what it means to settle.

Takahiro Yoshino

ZEN ROUND BACK CHAIR

As a furniture maker, the most significant thing I do is to give the maximum respect for the life of the trees I use, making concessions to the wood as the beauty of the wood reveals itself. Traditional Japanese design is congruent with nature, expressing the inherent beauty in everyday design.

The most important aspect of my chairs is based on the practice of zazen sitting. Zazen is the experience of the harmony of body and soul that we seek to achieve in our daily life: a method of sitting where your head and pelvis are in perfect alignment, reducing the stress you encounter throughout the day.

I have developed a method of making personalized chairs that entails fitting the chair to the contours of the pelvis and spine thus promoting correct posture through zazen positioning. Both my chaise lounge and Zen chairs are an elegant unification of modern-day ergonomics, engineering, design, and traditional Japanese woodworking, craftsmanship, and Zen practices.

Zen Round Back Chair,
2015 | Japanese maple |
28 x 25 x 20 in.

Checklist of the Exhibition

Jennifer Anderson
Cadwalader Chair, 2016
Mud, steel
37 x 22 x 26 in.
Heather McCalla

Justin G. Bailey
Airliner Chair, 2015
Powder-coated steel, plywood, canvas
32 x 22 x 23 in.

Bob Brox
Entrenching [S]tool, 2015
Shovel handles, used tire rubber, cotter pins, washers, screws, oil finish
19 x 17 x 15 in.

Stoel Burrowes
"A" Back Windsor, 2012
White oak, ash, poplar,
oil and wax finish
38 x 27 x 20 in.

Stoel Burrowes
Metal Cat's Cradle, 2014
Metal, bungee seat and back
39 x 26 x 28 in.

Sheri Crider & Nina Dubois
Drift #1, 2015
Hollow-core doors, wood glue
10 x 12 x 16 ft.

Alicia Dietz
Reintegration, 2015
Oak pallets, audio, fabric, LED lighting
chair 26 x 26 x 28 in.; flooring
6 x 10 x 16 ft.
Jeremy Zietz

Jack R. Elliott
Triakonta25—WBC, 2010
Cast aluminum, stainless steel,
black locust
32 x 18 x 24 in.

Dugan Essick
Geisha Bar Stool, 2015
Marine mahogany, carbon fiber
44 x 21 x 24 in.

Adrian Ferrazzutti
Signature Arm Chair, 2012
Hickory, leather
35 x 25 x 29 in.

Adrian Ferrazzutti
Fallingbrook Chair, 2012
Ash, wenge
32 x 18 x 22 in.

Adrian Ferrazzutti
Baleen Chair, 2013
Wenge, satin wood
29 x 28 x 26 in.

Amy Forsyth
Treehouse Chair, 2015–2016
Basswood, paint, fabric
68 x 35 x 25 in.

Jordan Gehman
Booster, 2012
Found chair, mahogany, paint
25 x 13 x 13 in.

Sophie Glenn
Collapsible Stools, 2015
Various woods and
powder-coated steel
18–22 x 12–14 in. dia.

Sophie Glenn
School Desk, 2015
Walnut and painted steel
30 x 24 x 35 in.

Tad Gloeckler
Segment Rotation Seat, 2005
Birch-veneer plywood, stainless steel,
threaded rod
15 x 30 x 20 in.

Doug Jones & Carrie Compton
The Ninth Chair: Beyond Burnt, 2015
Alder, white oak, wax
40 x 20 x 21 in.
Margot Geist, Geistlight Photography

Lauren Kalman
But if the Crime Is Beautiful …
Composition with Ornament
and Object, 2014
Inkjet print
20 x 16 in.

Patrick Kana
Incrementum, 2015
Soft maple, limestone
72 x 16 x 13
Elizabeth Torgerson-Lamark

David Knopp
Chair, 2015
Baltic birch, plywood
32 x 60 x 36 in.

Beth Krensky
Portable Sanctuary #1, Performance
Video, 2012
Video

Joseph G. La Macchia
Continuum Chair, 2014
Urban walnut
30 x 22 x 24 in.

Jack Larimore
re-pair, 2008
Douglas fir
52 x 68 x 32 in.

Po Shun Leong
Fortune Cookie Stool, 2008
Bent laminated polywood, paint
18½ x 19 x 18 in.

Laura Mays
Ample, 2015
Ash, narra, upholstery
46 x 28 x 32 in.

Christine Mei
Shapeshifter, 2015
Plywood
30 x 30 x 20 in.

Taiji Miyasaka
Skinny Love Chair, 2011
Oak
32 x 16¾ x 18½ in.

Mira Nakashima
Concordia Chair, 2003
American black walnut
31½ x 19½ x 16 in.

Christy Oates
Facet Chair, 2012
Plywood, maple and
sapele wood veneers
16 x 16 x 33 in.

Keunho Peter Park
Cocoon Chair, 2013
Cherry
59 x 72 x 156 in.

Gord Peteran
Electric Chair, 2006
Metal, bulb
36 x 14 x 18 in.

Dean Pulver
Memorial Bench, 2008
Bleached ash
110 x 58 x 58 in.

Andrew Jay Rumpler
Tatum's Lounge, 2010
Recycled piano keys, resin and glass
fiber, steel
29½ x 18½ x 23 in.

Fabiano Sarra
Spada Chair, 2012
Ebonized ash, white oak, brass
24 x 22 x 18 in.

Matt Selnick
Strobo, 2015
Taskboard, primer, paint
5½ x 2¾ x 4¼ in.

Mark Sfirri
Pally Ludie, 2014
White pine
16½ x 10¾ x 10¾ in.

Mark Sfirri
Chubbette, 2014
White pine
13½ x 36 x 10½ in.

Mark Sfirri
Lady Whistle, 2015
White pine
18 x 11 x 11 in.

Michaela Crie Stone
Seated Springbok, 2015
Maple, springbok hair-on hide
28 x 24 x 36 in.

Michaela Crie Stone
Gigi Chair, 2015
Maple, steel
28 x 18 x 26 in.

Joshua Torbick
Wedged In, 2015
Walnut, steel, leather
25 x 16 x 45 in.

Joshua Torbick
Restructured Chair, 2015
Ash
24 x 19 x 43 in.

Misha Volf
4 x 4 Bench, 2015
Eastern red cedar, ratchet straps
32 x 60 x 31 in.

Takahiro Yoshino
Zen Round Back Chair, 2015
Japanese maple
28 x 25 x 20 in.

Artists' Bios

JENNIFER ANDERSON

Jennifer Anderson started her education at UC Davis, where she completed a BS in environmental design (1995). Upon graduating from Davis, she trained as a fine cabinetmaker at the College of the Redwoods (2000), studying under master craftsman James Krenov. She then went on to earn an MFA from San Diego State University (2006), where she studied under Wendy Maruyama.

Currently, Jennifer divides her time between her studio art practice and teaching at Palomar College in San Marcos, California, and other institutions, including Anderson Ranch Arts Center in Snowmass Village, Colorado, and Haystack Mountain School of Crafts in Deer Isle, Maine. Her art is exhibited nationally and internationally and can be seen in publications including *Interior Design* and *American Craft*. Jennifer has been the Windgate Artist in Residence at both San Diego State University and the University of Wisconsin–Madison.

JUSTIN G. BAILEY

Justin G. Bailey is currently an MFA candidate in 3-D design in 2016. Previously, Justin studied at Webster University, where he received a BFA in sculpture in 2008.

Justin has a varied professional background that has helped inform the evolution of his work. While an undergraduate, Justin worked in museum operations at Laumeier Sculpture Park in Saint Louis, Missouri, where he helped build furniture for the first time. Justin currently teaches undergraduate design and modeling courses at the University of Iowa and just spent the summer working in interior design at Sasaki Associates in Boston.

In 2014 Justin worked with a group of 3-D design students from the University of Iowa to create the school's interactive installation at SOFA Chicago, which took first place among exhibiting universities through SOFA's Connect program. In 2015 Justin was a student NICHE Award finalist and exhibited pieces at the SaloneSatellite in Milan and ICFF in New York.

BOB BROX

Bob Brox is a civil engineer working on water and sanitation projects for refugees and displaced people. He also enjoys woodworking and in particular making tables and chairs, and has been lucky enough to sell a few pieces and win some awards. Working all over the developing world has had a profound influence on his furniture, which is generally sparse and unadorned.

He grew up in Massachusetts and studied at the University of Massachusetts, Amherst (BS civil engineering, 1988) and at Johns Hopkins (master of public health, 1996). He currently lives in Valence, France, with his wife and son.

STOEL BURROWES

Since 2000 Stoel Burrowes has been on the faculty of the Department of Interior Architecture at the University of North Carolina, Greensboro. In that time, he has also taught at Virginia Commonwealth University in Richmond, Virginia, in the Department of Interior Design. He has also taught at Maryland Institute College of Art in Baltimore, Maryland. He pursues chairmaking as research, skill, and avocation.

His education includes fifteen years of furniture making, design, and sales. He holds a master's degree in industrial design from North Carolina State University (1994). He earned a BA in history of art from Yale University (1975).

His chairs have won Golden A' Design Awards in 2011 and 2012.

CARRIE COMPTON
(COLLABORATING WITH DOUG JONES)

Carrie Compton studied woodworking/furniture design and printmaking at Santa Fe Community College from 2011 to 2015, where she completed the certificate program in fine woodworking. Before she discovered her love of woodworking, she obtained a bachelor of arts degree in fine arts / art history and a master's of business administration from the University of New Mexico. She has exhibited in both fine woodworking and printmaking shows in Santa Fe.

SHERI CRIDER
(COLLABORATING WITH NINA DUBOIS)

Sheri Crider lives and works in Albuquerque, New Mexico.

Born in Phoenix, Arizona, Sheri is a contemporary artist focused on creating sculptural objects/installations that repurpose materials. She has created several series of drawings that are thought of as an additional means to record a rapidly changing environment. Sheri received a BFA from the University of Arizona and an MFA from the University of New Mexico (2001).

ALICIA DIETZ

Alicia Dietz served in the US Army for ten years as an officer, Blackhawk maintenance test pilot, and company commander. She flew combat and peacekeeping missions in Iraq, and was stationed in Alaska, Egypt, Israel, and Europe.

After the military, Alicia studied traditional woodworking at Vermont Woodworking School, where she was mentored by Garrett Hack. She interned with Wendy Maruyama, and is currently earning her MFA at Virginia Commonwealth University.

Alicia has received numerous awards, including the Virginia Museum of Fine Arts Visual Arts Fellowship; Niche Award (finalist); Emerging Artist and Innovators VMFA Gift Shop Product Award; Vermont Fine Furniture and Design Competition Best in Show and two Student First Place awards and one Best in show at Vermont Fine Furniture and Design Competition; the Robert Fletcher Memorial Award; and scholarships from The Furniture Society, Haystack, Penland, Anderson Ranch, Corning Museum of Glass, and Arrowmont.

Her current work is the beginning of a journey to expose the visible and invisible wounds of veterans and to explore her thoughts about what war does to soldiers' bodies, to their minds, and to their humanity.

NINA DUBOIS
(COLLABORATING WITH SHERI CRIDER)

Nina Dubois incorporates aspects of art, architecture, and design to generate spaces that allow for alternative understandings and experiences of the environments we inhabit. She has participated in programs, residencies, and events that aim to dissolve the boundaries between art, life, and landscape, such as the Land Arts of the American West program; ISEA: Machine Wilderness; and the 2013 edition of the High Desert Test Sites.

Nina received a BFA with honors from Concordia University in Montreal and an MFA with distinction with a concentration in art and ecology from the University of New Mexico (2014). She was selected for the Marion Monical Memorial Scholarship and the Phyllis Muth Scholarship for Fine Arts, both from the Department of Art & Art History, UNM. Nina has been working as an art educator, most recently as visiting faculty for foundations at UNM, and is currently developing education programs at the Canadian Center for Architecture in Montreal.

JACK R. ELLIOTT

Jack R. Elliott is an associate professor at Cornell University where he teaches studios on design and conducts research on environmental issues in the built environment. Since he began at Cornell in 1998, Jack uses the prototype situated in a real world context to stimulate design discourse, pull technology, and provide possibilities for commercial enterprise. He earned a bachelor's degree in physics with a minor in sculpture at the University of Alberta (1978), as well as two master's degrees, one in architecture (1991) and one in product design (1993), from the University of Calgary. Over the years, Jack has won numerous awards for teaching, research, and design. Most recently, he has won recognitions for his sculptural works, including the 2015 Atkinson Center for Sustainable Futures Residency Fellowship at Cornell, the 2014 Leon Andrus Award for Best in Show from the Adkins Arboretum, and the 2013 Award of Excellence from the Memorial Art Gallery, Rochester, New York.

DUGAN ESSICK

Dugan Essick graduated in 1974 from San Francisco State College with a degree in industrial arts, emphasis on wood. In 2000, he moved to Grass Valley, California, to build and open his woodworking school (Essick Woodworking School). He is now spending his time equally teaching furniture making and building new designs of his own.

ADRIAN FERRAZZUTTI

Adrian Ferrazzutti lives and work in Guelph, Ontario, and has over fifteen years of professional experience as a maker of fine furniture and decorative wooden objects. He graduated in 1998 from the Fine Woodworking Program at the College of the Redwoods in California, where he studied for two years with James Krenov. The Canada Council for the Arts has awarded him several grants, and his work has been exhibited in cities across Canada and in the United States, including Toronto, New York, and Chicago. His work has been widely published in books and magazines, and he is a contributing writer for *Fine Woodworking* magazine, which recently released a DVD on his box-making technique. He also teaches fine woodworking at schools in Canada and the US. He works independently as well as in collaboration with architects to create unique work for private residences.

AMY FORSYTH

Amy Forsyth started out studying music, then moved to architecture, where she remained long enough to get two degrees and begin a university teaching career. Then, she fell in love with furniture, and ever since, has been designing and building furniture and similar artifacts when she's not teaching or playing her fiddle. She is an associate professor of art, architecture, and design at Lehigh University and performs with several bands in the Berks County and Lehigh Valley area.

JORDAN GEHMAN

Jordan Gehman is an artist and furniture maker currently residing in Madison, Wisconsin. He earned his BFA in woodworking from the Maine College of Art and his MFA in furniture design from San Diego State University. Jordan has been an artist in residence at Oregon College of Art and Craft, the Center for Furniture Craftsmanship, Indiana University of Pennsylvania, and The Center for Art in Wood. He has been published in books and magazines, and has exhibited nationally and internationally. His hobbies include documenting and collecting discarded furniture, dismantling things with no intention of putting them back together, riding bikes, and continually exploring the relationships between humans and objects.

SOPHIE GLENN

Born and raised in New York City, Sophie Glenn received her BFA in sculpture at SUNY Purchase College (2012), where she also worked as a teaching assistant for sculpture, metal, and bronze casting courses. After graduating, she worked as a metal fabricator and welder for Shelton Studios Inc. in Brooklyn, New York, and as a studio assistant for Vivian Beer at Vivian Beer Studio Works in Manchester, New Hampshire. She is currently pursuing her MFA in furniture design and woodworking (2016), as well as teaching foundations and introductory woodworking courses, at San Diego State University.

TAD GLOECKLER

Tad Gloeckler is an associate professor in the Lamar Dodd School of Art at the University of Georgia in Athens, Georgia. Tad earned his master's of architecture from the University of Wisconsin–Milwaukee in 1987. He has taught architecture and interior design programs for twenty years and was in architectural practice for nearly ten years prior to teaching. Before starting his career in design, Tad worked on conservation initiatives with the National Forest / Park Service and Fisheries Departments. He has won numerous awards in national and international art and design venues.

DOUG JONES
(COLLABORATING WITH CARRIE COMPTON)

Doug Jones graduated in 1992 from Rhode Island School of Design with an MFA in furniture design. He also holds a BA from Wesleyan University (1982) and completed the Fine Woodworking program at Bucks County Community College.

He is currently an assistant professor at Santa Fe Community College, where he coheads the Fine Woodworking program. Previously he was the program head of woodworking at the Shelburne Craft School near Burlington, Vermont. Since 1992, Doug and his wife, Kim Kulow-Jones, have operated Random Orbit Studio.

Doug received an Award of Excellence from the American Association of Woodturners in 2009; Best in Show, Vermont Fine Furniture and Design Competition in 2006; and an Award of Achievement at the San Francisco American Craft Council Show in 2004.

LAUREN KALMAN

Lauren Kalman is a visual artist whose practice is invested in contemporary craft, video, photography, and performance. Lauren's work has been featured in exhibitions at the Renwick Gallery at the Smithsonian Museum of American Art, Museum of Contemporary Craft, Museum of Arts and Design, Cranbrook Art Museum, Contemporary Art Museum Houston, Mint Museum, and the deCordova Museum, among others. Her work is in the permanent collection of the Museum of Fine Arts Boston and the Smithsonian Museum of American Art.

She has been awarded residencies at the Bemis Center, Australian National University, Corporation of Yaddo, Virginia Center for Creative Arts, Brush Creek Arts Foundation, and Haystack, among others. Her awards include Ludwig Vogelstein Foundation, Puffin Foundation West, and ISE Cultural Foundation Emerging Curator grants.

PATRICK KANA

As a sailor and a son of two marine biologists, Patrick Kana tries to focus his love for the natural world through an act of making. A maker of sorts since he was a young boy, he continued formal training in luthiery, furniture making, and sculpture through two long-term apprenticeships and college. He was a 2010 recipient of the Powermatic Workshop Scholarship, and in 2012 was a workshop assistant at the Penland School of Craft and the Center for Furniture Craftsmanship. After establishing his own studio practice, he returned to school for his MFA in furniture design at the School for American Craft at RIT, later graduating in 2015. He has had work selected for the permanent collections at both Hobart and William Smith Colleges and the Rochester Institute of Technology, and continues to make furniture and sculpture for galleries and on commission.

DAVID KNOPP

David Knopp resides in Baltimore, Maryland. He attended Essex Community College and Towson University. In 2012 David received the Mary Sawyer Baker Artist Award, which included an exhibit at the Baltimore Museum of Art. He was a recipient of the Maryland State Art Council's Individual Artist Award in 2012. In 2013 he was a semifinalist for the Sondheim Prize. Since then he has been invited to exhibit work throughout the Baltimore and Philadelphia metropolitan areas.

He was accepted in juried exhibitions including Craftforms 2011–2014, Living with Craft Invitational 2014, SOFA Chicago 2014, and Delaware Center for Contemporary Art 2013 and 2014. One of his sculpted chairs is in the permanent collection of the American Visionary Art Museum.

BETH KRENSKY

Beth Krensky is an associate professor of art education at the University of Utah. She received a BFA from the Boston Museum School and Tufts University (1988), a master's in education from the Harvard Graduate School of Education (1991), and a PhD from the University of Colorado–Boulder (2002). She has exhibited widely throughout the United States and internationally. She is a founding member of the international artist collective the Artnauts and is a fellow with the Jewish Art Salon, New York City. She has received multiple teaching and research awards, including the University of Utah Early Career Teaching Award, the University of Utah Public Service Professorship, the College of Fine Arts Faculty Excellence Award in Research, and the University of Utah Presidential Scholar Award.

JOSEPH G. LA MACCHIA

Joseph G. La Macchia is classically trained in the most ancient sense of the phrase. Like thousands of generations of artists who have come before, his education is equal parts observation, apprenticeship, and experimentation.

As a boy, he spent countless afternoons with his grandfather in his woodshop. His grandfather's inventiveness fed Joseph's desire to make things. He would watch his grandfather and then go take his toys apart and invent new ones. As he grew, he was drawn toward tools of other disciplines: the pencil and the brush; the lens and the landscape; the potter's wheel and the farmer's plow. He would take classes here and there to learn fundamentals or refine technique, but no matter where his artisanal mind took him, his artist's heart always brought him back to the plane and the chisel, the wood and the saw.

JACK LARIMORE

Jack Larimore grew up in the cherry orchard region of northeastern Michigan. He attended Michigan State University, earning a degree in landscape architecture in 1973. Since 1983, Jack has been self-employed as a sculptor and furniture maker. His work has been exhibited internationally and is included in major private and public collections. Additionally, he has served as a professor in the Crafts Department at the University of the Arts in Philadelphia, as an advisory board member of The Furniture Society, as a trustee for The Center for Art in Wood, and as a board member at Wheaton Arts and Cultural Center. Jack is featured in the recently released book *Furniture with Soul* by David Savage (Kodansha International).

PO SHUN LEONG

After several positions in British architects' offices, the first job that changed Po Shun Leong's direction was with an American Friends Service Committee project as a volunteer in a Mexican village. Cuauhtenco is a remote community high up on the side of a volcano. The villagers wove intricate blankets, and Po Shun became their student weaver of medium velocity.

With sixteen years' experience making furniture of the affordable kind in Mexico, Po Shun relocated to southern California in 1981. Expecting to continue with furniture, Po Shun got caught up in a period of intricately complex sculptural wood art that lasted until around 2007.

Since the return to purely functional furniture, the designs look easy on the eye when in fact simple can make life difficult.

LAURA MAYS

Laura Mays graduated with a degree in architecture from University College Dublin in 1992, but found that she yearned for a more hands-on making experience than architecture allows. Subsequently she trained in woodworking and furniture design at GMIT Letterfrack in Ireland in 1996 and at the College of the Redwoods in California in 2003. She also earned a master's in design from NCAD in Dublin, Ireland, in 2010. She works as a professional furniture designer-maker and teacher and is the program director of the Fine Woodworking Program at College of the Redwoods in Fort Bragg, California. Her work is in the collection of the National Museum of Ireland and personal collections in Ireland and the United States.

Index

Schiffer Publishing
 Designer: Justin Watkinson
 Design Director: John Cheek
 Managing Editor: Catherine Mallette
 Editor: Sandra Korinchak
 Copyeditor: Alex Potter
 Production Purchasing: Pamela Shumway-Bilak

The Center for Art in Wood
 Managing Editor: Judson Randall, Oceanside, Oregon
 Copyeditor: Anne McPeak, Brooklyn, New York
 Creative Director: Dan Saal, StudioSaal Corporation, Oakland, California
 Designer: Alvaro Villanueva, Oakland, California
 Project Coordinator: Karen Schoenewaldt

Type set in Ideal Sans, designed by Hoefler & Co.

ISBN: 978-0-7643-5169-3
Printed in China

Published by Schiffer Publishing, Ltd.
4880 Lower Valley Road | Atglen, PA 19310
Phone: (610) 593-1777; Fax: (610) 593-2002
E-mail: Info@schifferbooks.com
Web: www.schifferbooks.com

For our complete selection of fine books on this and related subjects, please visit our website at www.schifferbooks.com. You may also write for a free catalog.

Schiffer Publishing's titles are available at special discounts for bulk purchases for sales promotions or premiums. Special editions, including personalized covers, corporate imprints, and excerpts, can be created in large quantities for special needs. For more information, contact the publisher.

We are always looking for people to write books on new and related subjects. If you have an idea for a book, please contact us at proposals@schifferbooks.com.

The Center for Art in Wood
141 N. 3rd Street | Philadelphia, PA 19106
Phone: (215) 923-8000
Web: www.centerforartinwood.org

This book is published on the occasion of the exhibition *On the Edge of Your Seat: Chairs for the 21st Century,* on view at The Center for Art in Wood from May 6–July 23, 2016.

The Center for Art in Wood will continue to be the preeminent arts and education organization advancing the growth, awareness, appreciation and promotion of artists and the creation and design of art in wood and wood in combination with other materials.

The exhibition and publication are produced by The Center for Art in Wood. Contact the Center for more information on this publication or exhibition, other publications produced by the Center, or about the art of wood.

Every reasonable attempt has been made to identify owners of copyright. Errors or omission will be corrected in subsequent editions.

Prologue "The Clan of the Cave Crafts" by Roy Superior courtesy of Mara Superior

Front Cover:
Windsor armchair, 1770–1800 | Soft maple, tulip poplar, white oak, hickory, paint | Pennsylvania | Winterthur Museum, bequest of Henry Francis du Pont, 1959.1634
Mira Nakashima | *Concordia Chair,* 2003 | see p. 214

Back Cover:
Armchair, 1760–1775 | see p. 40
Lauren Kalman | *But if the Crime Is Beautiful,* 2014 | see p. 172

Endpapers:
Jennifer Anderson | *Cadwalader Chair,* 2016 | see p. 116
Jack Larimore | *re-pair,* 2008 | see p. 192

Images on Pages in Red:
p. 2 | Fabiano Sarra | *Spada Chair,* 2012 | see p. 234
p. 4 | Mark Sfirri | *Pally Ludie,* 2014 | see p. 242
p. 6 | Dugan Essick | *Geisha Bar Stool,* 2015 | see p. 142
p. 7 | Joshua M. Torbick | *Restructured Chair,* 2015 | see p. 252
p. 12 | Michaela Crie Stone | *Gigi Chair,* 2015 | see p. 246
p. 13 | Doug Jones & Carrie Compton | *The Ninth Chair: Beyond Burnt,* 2015 | see p. 168
p. 85 | Takahiro Yoshino | *Zen Round Back Chair,* 2015 | see p. 260
p. 87 | Joseph G. La Macchia | *Continuum Chair,* 2014 | see p. 188
p. 115 | Jennifer Anderson | *Cadwalader Chair,* 2016 | see p. 116
p. 264 | Stoel Burrowes | *Metal Cat's Cradle,* 2014 | see p. 128
p. 265 | Justin G. Bailey | *Airliner Chair,* 2015 | see p. 120
p. 279 | Adrian Ferrazzutti | *Baleen Chair,* 2013 | see p. 146